HOW WE WRITE

HOW WE WRITE

THIRTEEN WAYS OF LOOKING AT A BLANK PAGE

EDITED BY
SUZANNE CONKLIN AKBARI

A publication of the DEAD LETTER OFFICE via

punctum books (P) brooklyn, n.y.

HOW WE WRITE
© 2015 Suzanne Conklin Akbari

First published in 2015 by
Dead Letter Office, BABEL Working Group
an imprint of punctum books
Brooklyn, New York
http://punctumbooks.com
http://babelworkinggroup.org

The BABEL Working Group is a collective and desiring-assemblage of scholar-gypsies with no leaders or followers, no top and no bottom, and only a middle. BABEL roams and stalks the ruins of the post-historical university as a multiplicity, a pack, looking for other roaming packs and multiplicities with which to cohabit and build temporary shelters for intellectual vagabonds. We also take in strays.

ISBN-13: 978-0692519332
ISBN-10: 0692519335

Cover art: Detail of *Wabi Sabi Agnes Martin*,
         Yvonne Wiegers (yvonnewiegers.ca).
Facing-page drawing: Heather Masciandaro.
Book design: Chris Piuma.

Before you start to read this book,

take this moment to think about making a donation to punctum books, an independent non-profit press,

@ http://punctumbooks.com/about/

If you're reading the e-book, you can click on the image below to go directly to our donations site. Any amount, no matter the size, is appreciated and will help us to keep our ship of fools afloat. Contributions from dedicated readers will also help us to keep our commons open and to cultivate new work that can't find a welcoming port elsewhere. Our adventure is not possible without your support. Vive la open-access.

Fig. 1. Hieronymus Bosch, Ship of Fools (1490-1500)

Table of Contents

Introduction
Written Chatter and
the Writer's Voice

> Among twenty snowy mountains,
> The only moving thing
> Was the eye of the blackbird.
> > —Wallace Stevens, "Thirteen Ways of
> > Looking at a Blackbird"

When we write, we write alone. Being alone means control, productive solitude, introspective bliss; it also means loneliness, isolation, even fear. Our writing environments have, however, become intensely social through the emergence of a range of online platforms, including websites and blogs but also including more casual and short-form media, such as Facebook and Twitter. The much lamented decline in the circulation of hand-written letters has given way to ubiquitous written "chatter," which simultaneously nourishes the lonely writer and threatens to distract her from her "real" writing.

This little book emerges from that world of written chatter. Following a roundtable discussion on dissertation-writing, organized by me and hosted by the School of Graduate Studies at the University of Toronto, one of the participants—Michael Collins—wrote a wonderful blog post that arose from the roundtable but moved beyond its scope to address the conditions of writing more generally, including not only the emotional and intellectual demands posed by the task but the real, material

IMAGE: On the deck of the schooner *Hindu*, Provincetown Harbor, July 2015.

conditions of academic writing in graduate school.[1] Michael's thoughtful engagement with his own experience of writing—posted and reposted on a number of Facebook pages—led to an outpouring of personal accounts of the dissertation-writing years, both from those currently in the trenches and those for whom those years are very much in the rear-view mirror. What emerged was a clear sense of the diversity of writing practices that are out there: there's no single "right" way to write, and exposure to that range of practices might help those who are in the process of mastering academic writing to feel more confident in their own abilities, most of all by demonstrating that such "mastery" is an ongoing—potentially limitless—effort.

Like the thirteen verses of Wallace Stevens' poem, which gives this book its subtitle and epigraph, what follows is thirteen individual yet related parts that make up a single whole. Each essay refracts its writer's experience, generating a spectrum of perspectives where much common ground appears—and much variety. This is how it came into being: in response to Michael Collins's blog post and the ensuing written chatter (especially on Facebook), Alexandra Gillespie and I wrote a joint post, generously hosted by Jeffrey Cohen and his collaborators at the In the Middle blog, titled "How Do We Write? Dysfunctional Academic Writing."[2] I was fascinated by the way that this conversation seemed to strike a nerve for many readers, both across the blogs and on Facebook, and therefore decided to try to find a way to gather some of this material to make it more readily available. I began to ask colleagues whether they might be willing to contribute some thoughts on their own writing process for a very short volume, having

1   http://nfldtxt.com/2015/05/26/wilderness-group-tour-phd-dissertations-and-writingsupportaccountablity-groups/

2   http://www.inthemedievalmiddle.com/2015/05/how-do-we-write-dysfunctional-academic.html

heard from a number of people that such a collection might be useful—not in describing how *to* write, but how we actually do write.

Based on input from friends, colleagues, and students, I decided that what would be most useful would be a very short volume, with about a dozen contributors each providing an essay of 2000–3000 words. Wondering what sort of range of contributors to include, I asked grad students and recent graduates, who said that what they found particularly useful were accounts by more experienced writers—not exactly the same as senior scholars, as this could also include those with ample writing experience before the PhD, or who concurrently write in other modes. Accordingly, the contributors range from graduate students and recent PhDs to senior scholars, working in the fields of medieval studies, art history, English literature, poetics, early modern studies, musicology, and geography. All are engaged in academic writing, but some of the contributors also publish in other genres, including poetry and fiction. Several contributors maintain a very active online presence, including blogs and websites; all are committed to strengthening the bonds of community, both in person and online, which helps to explain the effervescent sense of collegiality that pervades the volume, creating linkages across essays and extending outward into the wide world of writers and readers.

The dissertation-writing roundtable I mentioned took place on 25 May 2015; Michael's blog post appeared on 26 May, and the joint blog post by Alex and me appeared on 30 May; another participant in the roundtable, Alice Hutton Sharp, also wrote up her reflections, published on her blog on 5 June.[3] As I write this,

---

3 https://theaccidentalphilologist.wordpress.com/2015/06/05/
the-community-you-have-the-community-you-need-building-
an-online-accountability-group/

reading over the essays submitted by the contributors—some still in draft form, some appearing in draft as blog posts over the last few weeks—it is mid-July. In other words, this book is the product of conversation, *is* itself part of a conversation, emerging from a rapidly proliferating series of short-form writing on the topic of how we write. One commentary generated another, each one characterized by enormous speed, eloquence, and emotional forthrightness. This collection is not about how *to* write, but how *we* write: unlike a prescriptive manual that promises to unlock the secret to efficient productivity, the contributors talk about their own writing processes, in all their messy, frustrated, exuberant, and awkward glory.

As noted above, this collection has grown by accretion, which is an unconventional but (I think) interesting organizational strategy. It was inspired by the language of a Facebook post by Michael Collins where he linked to the guest blog post that had just been published on In the Middle, using the metaphor of the pebble and the landslide. Michael introduced his link to the post by Alex and me this way:

> Respected tenured scholars who binge write, whose writing practices are "wrong" just as many grad students' are—except they aren't wrong at all. The idea that writing is personal and no one writing practice is "correct"—and a good writing practice is built on self-knowledge. This sprung from that blog post I put up last week. Posting something on a blog is kind of like pushing a pebble down a mountain. Often it just clatters down all alone. But sometimes other pebbles join and it becomes a wonderful landslide and here the metaphor breaks down. But I guess I bring this up because: we are never writing into a void even if it sometimes feels that way. Writing is a social act. You never know how that pebble is gonna bounce.

Spurred on by this comment, I asked Michael if we could use his "pebble"—that is, his blog post—as the first essay in the group, followed by me and Alex, and then others in roughly the order that they participated in the conversation, starting with Alice Hutton Sharp's blog post, which also emerged from the 25 May roundtable. The Table of Contents, accordingly, demarcates the ripples in the pond that arose from the pebble of Michael's blog post: contributors were invited because they had commented on one of the posts, or because they had reposted a link with additional comments, or simply because the conversation had led to their virtual door.

I began by asking Jeffrey Cohen, Asa Mittman, Maura Nolan, and Rick Godden to make contributions, all four of whom had responded in interesting ways to the initial blog posts, and their responses and comments led, in turn, to other potential contributors. Jeffrey's essay focuses on how his perspective on writing practices has changed since he wrote a 2011 blog post on this topic, and its own accretive style—moving from the 2011 post to a series of "writing lockdown" status updates from 2013, and finally to a reflection from the present moment—is a microcosm of the accretive style of this volume as a whole. Asa writes about the process of collaborative writing, a format that he has particularly embraced in spite of the fact that the bureaucratic administrative processes around hiring, tenure, and promotion in humanities fields are generally ill-equipped to evaluate collaborative work. Asa and I have very different writing styles, as we discovered (!) when we wrote an article together last year; his essay here has helped me to understand how helpful it is for all of us to have a frank discussion about writing practices, to share our common expectations and idiosyncrasies, before embarking on joint projects.

Maura Nolan and Rick Godden have contributed essays that bring out their experiences of teaching writing, both to graduates and undergraduates, and the ways that individual life experiences—especially as they change over time—inflect our own writerly practices. Bruce Holsinger and Steve Mentz contribute essays from the perspective of writers who are deeply engaged in academic writing, but who also write in other modes—Bruce being a prolific writer of fiction, and Steve integrating poetry into his literary production. Steve also draws out the intersection of blogging, seascape environments, and longer-form academic writing. Stuart Elden—whose regular blogging and writing about his work in progress have nourished my own writing practice—describes his accretive or "accumulative" writing style, which involves putting together little bits of writing into bigger forms. Like Stuart, Derek Gregory describes his work in progress through blogging, and has written in the past about his practice of integrating oral and written formats, using the act of speaking publicly to develop a written text. Dan Kline lays out a series of "lessons" that emerge from his own writerly life—that is, the ways in which his writing process has evolved as his life has taken different turns, and the way that writing has served as a means to process the experience of change over time. Throughout, the accretive mode of writing has underlain the overall development of this collection, just as it has underlain the writing practice of many of our contributors—as described in Jeffrey and Stuart's essays, and in the foundational metaphor coined by Michael Collins. This "landslide" has taken on a dynamic of its own, made up of many falling pebbles.

But—to be clear—the accretive mode of writing is not the only way to write. My own contribution, below, describes a method that could be aptly described as "put off writing until you can't avoid it any more, then hide yourself and do nothing else until the writing is done." I would not recommend this model to others, not just because it seems like a terrible idea but because I am—and have always been—ashamed of it. This fact became clear to me only when an insightful comment on the ITM blog post drew attention to the "self-deprecating" quality of what I had written, "to the point of self-contempt." The comment elicited more conversation on this "self-contempt" from both Alex and me, as follows:

8 June 2015
10:50 AM
Alexandra Gillespie said…
On self-contempt—well, it's real right? For whatever reason I don't experience it with respect to my writing practice and never did—but heaps of people do (and I experience it in other places in my academic life). Almost all my PhD supervisees exhibit some degree of self-loathing about their writing practice. It's quite something to see someone as established as Suzanne express the feeling honestly, and yet lightly. The lightness is critical: the difference between my younger and older selves' self-contempt, is that when younger it was cripplingly painful. Now it's more, wryly amused. I find my pathologies endearing—I like them, bc I like myself (most of the time). Suzanne has to speak for herself, but it seems to me that she doesn't take her self-contempt, any more than she takes herself, overly seriously. When I say—practice patience and empathy with yourself, I'd say, for god's sake don't beat yourself up for beating yourself up, if you can help it, bc you can't help it! Chillax about being totally not chillaxed! And other paradoxes.

11:01 AM
Suzanne Akbari said…
On self-contempt: it is real, and I think many of us have it. Alex is right that it can be crippling early on and becomes less so over time, but we still tend to hide it, even as established scholars. It emerges, I think, from the very habits of mind that make us good scholars: we judge, almost con-

stantly, the merit of work—the articles we read for research, the book ms we read for a press, abstract submissions, student work—and so naturally we judge ourselves as well. This is a good thing, because we hold ourselves to the same high standard we hold others. But while with a ms review, a tenure file, or a student paper, we begin by praising the positive before turning to critique, we rarely stop to praise ourselves.

(Comments from ITM blog post "How Do We Write? Dysfunctional Academic Writing," 8 June 2015)

I reproduce these comments in full because they capture the flavor of the exchange: we learn from one another, with commentary feeding back to the writers, allowing us in turn to move to a new position. Maybe I will stop to praise the positive, next time; maybe I will stop assuming that this terrible, immature way of writing, which I long hoped I would grow out of, is a defect. And maybe the value of talking frankly about our own experiences of writing will nourish others in our communities as much as it nourishes ourselves.

A later comment in the same thread brought out the serendipity of our connections to one another, and the ways in which frank conversations about how we write can enrich both our own practice and our communities, not only on the ground but also in the online environment:

10:13 AM
Annelies Kamp said…
This post reached me by way of my sister. I am in Ireland; she is in New Zealand. The wonders of social media allowed her to connect me to this discussion. And as have others, I'd like to thank you for pursuing this thought about being dysfunctional and how productive it can be!

I too have had to learn to write my own way. In recent weeks there has been a series of short articles by fiction writers outlining how they write: in the middle of the night, first thing in the morning, only with sustenance, always with a ritual, never with a ritual. And so on. That gave me such heart. Despite having produced a few books and a number of articles that I am proud to call my own, I have often struggled with the idea that I should do it "better." Colleagues who advise me they are up late at night after the children have gone to bed, or first thing in the morning before their commute to campus, have always left me with a lingering sense of being somehow inadequate. That's not how I work; but I do work. And I love it when that work of writing is done in a way that feels right to me because that creates the conditions for my ideas, my little unique contribution, to take form.

I share these kinds of stories with my students as they struggle with their own sense of how to begin. So many resources do not, to me, give any sense of the embodied author. I would love to see resources flow from this discussion and I'd be delighted to support it in any way, shape or form. Thank you both, and to all who have contributed comments. Oh, and thanks Tina for connecting me :-).

Here, a complex web of connectivity underlies the online conversation: the writer and her sister, who directed her to the blog; the colleagues with whom she's spoken, recounting their experiences of how to fit the work of writing into the interstices of domestic obligation; her students, who also "struggle" with their writing process, and with whom the writer "share[s]" her own histories of writing; the writers of the blog post, and those who have commented. The antipodean sweep of the writer's opening phrase—"I am in Ireland; she is in New Zealand"—is mirrored in the geographical sweep of the essays collected here, ranging from Michael Collins's Newfoundland to Dan Kline's Alaska, through Canada, the US, and the UK, and passing through diverse landscapes and seascapes.

One striking common ground in these essays is their focus on not just *how* we write, but *where* we write. This is manifested in several of the illustrations that accompany the essays, and also in the vivid accounts of the physical environment in which writing takes place—sometimes in a peaceful, almost sacred space; sometimes in the midst of domestic chaos, or in any one of many transitory or liminal spaces. As Alice Sharp puts it: "I have written on trains, I have written in Tim Horton's surrounded by flirting pre-teens, I have written at the dining room table. I write this now on the porch of a relative's home." Even when writing takes place in a busy environment, "surrounded by flirting pre-teens" or (in Steve Mentz's account) with a "month-old son, red-faced and screaming" on your shoulder, there seems to be an inner solitude, a still center, that sustains the writing process. Paradoxically, it is when we are together, united in a strong sense of community, that we are able to find the inner solitude and sense of stability that enables the writing process.

It comes as no surprise, therefore, that the physical environment where writing takes place is a site of fecundity: for Jeffrey Cohen, writing takes place in the "the former nursery of our house, a room about the size of a walk-in closet"; for Steve Mentz, swimming time is also a kind of writing time, so that "Writing emerges from putting little bodies in contact with vast seas." Our writing space is a site where the creative imagination does its work, where we give definite form to argument, to close reading, to creative analogy, to the affective turn of phrase. We are alone, when we write; but when we feel alone, we can also feel paralyzed, hopeless, unable to begin.

That's what this book is for: not feeling alone. The written chatter of the various essays collected here is meant to stimulate more conversation about how *you* write, reiterating and reinscribing a shared sense of community. The pebbles that follow—from Michael Collins's initial intervention through the variegated shards and fragments that spilled out in its wake— make up a landslide in which you, Reader, are also involved. We are looking forward to hearing your chatter, spoken or written, in person or online, and listening to your writer's voice.

Suzanne Conklin Akbari
North Truro, July 2015

About the Images

The authors have each chosen an image to illustrate "where they write"—which they have interpreted broadly. Some took photographs of their desks (with windows, books, papers, and cats) or drew maps of their local coffeeshops. Others depicted their mental writing spaces and illustrated their avatar, their support network, or their lines of escape. Several images may seem obscure at first glance; most are clarified in the essays.

All images are by the authors except the following:

p. xxiv: Anonymous self-portrait, taken c. 1900.

p. xxvi: Detail from "Various Fluorescent Minerals" by Hannes Grobe, used under Creative Commons Attribution–Share Alike 2.5 Generic Licence.

p. 18: Detail from *Half a Flagon* by Olivia Beaumont, reproduced by courtesy of the artist (www.etsy.com/shop/beaumontstudio).

p. 58: Get-well card by Siobhan Dale, then aged 7.

p. 82: Detail from British Library Additional 5762, fol. 28r.

p. 118: Photo by Olivia Mentz, used with permission.

The interlocking lines of the cover art are from a detail of *Wabi Sabi Agnes Martin* by Yvonne Wiegers, reproduced by permission of the artist (yvonnewiegers.ca).

Many thanks to the photographers and artists for letting us include their work in this collection.

Who We Are

MICHAEL COLLINS is a PhD candidate in English at the University of Toronto. He reads Newfoundland's minor literature, interpreting manifestations and adaptations of its strange geopolitical history and its current queer position. He's afraid for the future of the academy. He keeps a blog at nfldtxt.com. His writing habit is like that of a hunter-gatherer, packing up necessary tools and heading out to one of a number of likely spots to forage or stalk. That's why he drew a map, which you can use if you also write like this and happen to be visiting.

SUZANNE CONKLIN AKBARI is Director of the Centre for Medieval Studies at the University of Toronto, but would rather be working on her new project on medieval ideas of periodization, "The Shape of Time," and/or lying on the beach in North Truro. Her books include *Seeing Through the Veil: Optical Theory and Medieval Allegory* (2004), *Idols in the East: European Representations of Islam and the Orient, 1100–1450* (2009), and three collections of essays; the most recent one is *A Sea of Languages: Rethinking the Arabic Role in Medieval Literary History* (2013). She is also a co-editor of the *Norton Anthology of World Literature*, 3rd ed., and a master of structured procrastination.

ALEXANDRA GILLESPIE is an Associate Professor of English and Medieval Studies at the University of Toronto. At the time she was writing this, she was also trying to write her way to the end of several projects, among them a study called *Chaucer's Books*, a "new adult" fantasy trilogy co-authored with a friend, and three digital exhibitions of images from medieval manuscripts. She was failing to write the last few paragraphs of an essay owed to a colleague. As usual.

ALICE HUTTON SHARP is an Andrew W. Mellon Foundation Postdoctoral Fellow in the History and Classical Studies department at McGill University. She is currently writing a book about the origins of the *Glossa Ordinaria* on Genesis while pursuing new research on the use of reason as a defining human characteristic in twelfth- and thirteenth-century theology. She blogs—very occasionally—at theaccidentalphilologist.wordpress.com.

ASA SIMON MITTMAN is Professor of Art History at California State University, Chico, author of *Maps and Monsters in Medieval England* (2006), co-author with Susan Kim of *Inconceivable Beasts: The Wonders of the East in the Beowulf Manuscript* (2013), and author and co-author of numerous articles on monstrosity and marginality. He co-edited with Peter Dendle the *Research Companion to Monsters and the Monstrous* (2012), and co-directs with Martin Foys *Virtual Mappa*. CAA, ICMA, Kress, Mellon, American Philosophical Society, and NEH have supported his research. He edits book series with Boydell and Brill, and is founding president of MEARCSTAPA and a founding member of the Material Collective.

JEFFREY JEROME COHEN is Professor of English and Director of Institute for Medieval & Early Modern Studies at George Washington University. He blogs at inthemedievalmiddle.com and a full bio may be found at jeffreyjeromecohen.net. His punctum projects include *Animal, Vegetable, Mineral: Ethics and Objects*; *Inhuman Nature*; *Burn After Reading*; and *Object Oriented Environs*.

WHO WE ARE

MAURA NOLAN teaches medieval literature at UC-Berkeley, where she also directs Berkeley Connect, a campus-wide program in which advanced graduate students mentor undergraduates (www.berkeleyconnect.berkeley.edu). Her first book, *John Lydgate and the Making of Public Culture*, was published by Cambridge in 2005. She has published widely on Chaucer, Gower, Langland, Lydgate, Maitland, Adorno, Aquinas, and a range of essays on medieval aesthetics, beauty, style, and sensation. Her current project focuses on sensory poetics in Chaucer and Gower.

RICHARD H. GODDEN is a Postdoctoral Teaching Fellow at Tulane University, and has published in *postmedieval* and *New Medieval Literatures*. He is also coauthor with Jonathan Hsy of "Analytical Survey: Encountering Disability in the Middle Ages." His current work focuses on the intersections between the political theology of the neighbor, temporality, and Disability Studies in medieval romance. He also works on the alliances between Digital Humanities and Disability Studies. He has presented numerous papers throughout the US on related subjects, and his research has been funded by the Newcomb College Institute, Tulane University, and Washington University. He is a founding member of the Grammar Rabble.

BRUCE HOLSINGER teaches in the Department of English and Creative Writing at the University of Virginia. He has written two historical novels, *A Burnable Book* (winner of the Fisher Prize) and *The Invention of Fire* (HarperCollins/William Morrow), both set in late medieval England. He is completing *Archive of the Animal: Science, Sacrifice, and the Parchment Inheritance* for the University of Chicago Press, and has just begun a Very Short Introduction for Oxford University Press on the subject of historical fiction. He reviews fiction and nonfiction for the *Washington Post* and has written for *Slate*, *The Nation*, and other national publications.

STUART ELDEN is Professor of Political Theory and Geography at University of Warwick and Monash Warwick Professor at Monash University. He is the author of five books including *The Birth of Territory* (University of Chicago Press, 2013). He has been involved in editing several collections of Henri Lefebvre's writings, and has edited or co-edited books on Kant, Foucault and Sloterdijk. His next book is *Foucault's Last Decade* (Polity Press, forthcoming 2016), and he is now working on its prequel, *Foucault: The Birth of Power*. He runs a blog at www.progressivegeographies.com and hopes to return soon to a project on territory in Shakespeare's plays.

DEREK GREGORY is Peter Wall Distinguished Professor and Professor of Geography at the University of British Columbia in Vancouver. Ever since *The Colonial Present: Afghanistan, Palestine, Iraq* (2004) his writing has focused on later modern war, and on the ways in which military violence both on the ground and from the air has—and has not—changed since 1914. He is currently completing two new books, *The Everywhere War* and *War Material,* and his latest research concerns the treatment and evacuation of combatant and civilian casualties from war zones, 1914–2014.

STEVE MENTZ is Professor of English at St. John's University in New York City. He is the author of *At the Bottom of Shakespeare's Ocean* (2009), *Romance for Sale in Early Modern England* (2006), and co-editor of *Rogues and Early Modern English Culture* (2004) and *The Age of Thomas Nashe* (2013). He has written articles on ecocriticism, Shakespeare, and maritime literature and curated an exhibition at the Folger Shakespeare Library, "Lost at Sea: The Ocean in the English Imagination, 1550–1750" (2010). His book, *Shipwreck Modernity: Ecologies of Globalization, 1550–1719*, is forthcoming in 2015 from the University of Minnesota Press.

DANIEL T. KLINE (PhD, Indiana University) is Professor and Director of English at the University of Alaska, Anchorage, where he specializes in medieval literature, literary theory, and digital medievalism. His current research concerns children, violence, and ethics in late medieval England. Recent essays include contributions to *Levinas and Medieval Literature* (Duquesne UP, 2009) and *The Texts and Contexts of Oxford, Bodleian Library, MS Laud Misc. 108* (Brill, 2011). He edited the *Continuum Handbook of Medieval British Literature* (Continuum, 2009), *Digital Gaming Re-Imagines the Middle Ages* (Routledge, 2014), and co-edited, with Gail Ashton, *Medieval Afterlives in Popular Culture* (Palgrave-Macmillan, 2012).

How We Write

Atwood territory

Very Rich People

TORONTO REFERENCE LIBRARY

ENGL. DEPT.

SUBWAY

SBUX

SBUX

N

BLOOR

U of T

MERCURIO

UNIVERSITY OF TORONTO

SUBWAY

INDIGO

More condos

(Secret path)

U of T

PRATT LIBRARY

ARCoffee

ROBARTS DOOM LIBRARY

SBUX

GYM

HARBORD

U of T

SO MANY CONDOS

KELLY LIBRARY

QUEEN'S PARK

RUN circles

U of T

RIP BACK CAMPUS

HART HOUSE

SBUX

SUBWAY

WELLESLEY

GAY CHURCH

GERSTEIN LIBRARY

! FUEL

Gov't mnt

PRESSE

2ND CUP

COLLEGE

BAY

SBUX

YONGE

sleep here

SBUX SUPERMARKT

CARLTON

HOSPITALS

SUBWAY

current #1 spot

SUBWAY

SBUX

SUB-WAY

not thing before

Good sushi

WHERE I WRITE

UNIVERSITY

JIMMY'S

TALLEST CONDO

SBUX

RYERSON UNIVERSITY

SBUX

GERRARD

SUBWAY

Religious ppl w/ mics

CHIPOTLE

DUNDAS

SUBWAY

ART GALLERY OF ONTARIO

(best thing in Toronto)

OCAD UNIVERSITY

EATON CENTRE (mall)

FOOD COURT

Toronto's attempt at a Times Square

NFLD 2014 KM

Michael Collins
Wilderness Group Tour

I am a senior PhD candidate in the University of Toronto's
English Department. My most important job, the reason I am
here, is to write a dissertation. Yet, like a great majority of my
peers, I have struggled with accomplishing this task in a timely
fashion. I have struggled to complete this task in a way that
doesn't feel isolating and poisonous to my mental health. Con-
ventional wisdom, at least around these parts, is that candidates
like myself (that is to say, typical PhD candidates) should join
peer-organized writing groups, sometimes conceptualized as
"accountability" groups. We are lost in the deep wilderness, with
faulty out-of-date maps and an inconsistent, half-broken radio.
We imagine we are banding together for reasons of survival, to
help each other find a way out of the mess we're jointly in. Yet
it rarely works out that way.

   I've been a member of three such groups since beginning
work on my dissertation, and I've been invited to join more. One
group met (still meets) weekly (usually), at a café on campus.
They set individual goals for the week ahead and review how
each member did (or did not) meet the goals set at the previous week's meeting. In short, this group of peers meets to hold
one another accountable (thus: "accountability group"). When
I was an active member, I found this group became more of
a coffee klatch, a welcome chance for casual face-time with
friend-colleagues—a chance to talk shop and to catch up on
departmental gossip (one reason I fell out of the habit of attending: the other members were not actually my department-mates,
so the gossip and shoptalk was often of little relevance to me).
I think such groups are very valuable, psychologically and socially.

Writing a dissertation is often very isolating and depressing, and any light in the wilderness is a precious thing to those who wander in the dark. But, as a means of ensuring I got the majority of my crap done, week to week to week to week, it didn't work well for me.

A second group met only a few times before melting away. This was more of a "writing lock-in" than an "accountability" group. A fellow candidate in my department emailed a wide range of her peers (myself included), asking if we'd be interested in booking a room in our department for the purposes of a group writing session — no conversation, no distractions, just three hours of fingers going click-clack on keyboards, followed by a decompression session at a nearby pub for any interested. This was brilliant — I responded very well to this format, and I got a huge chunk of writing done at the first such meeting. However, it almost immediately began to come apart at the seams — the group was large, and the question "when shall we meet again?" became an unmanageable one. Person A can't do this day, Person B can't do that time, and so on. Two more sessions happened, as far as I'm aware, each one with fewer attendees. The last one I went to, I showed up about 20 minutes after it was meant to have started, and there was no one there. Scheduling conflicts and the demands of labour outside of/beyond the dissertation (demanding labour necessary for tenuous survival, I must stress) torpedoed this group.

A third group is still extant, although dormant, and is more of a writing workshop. There are five members, and in the first six months of the group's existence we tried to meet every six weeks or so (it was sometimes seven or eight weeks). A few days before a meeting, two or three pre-selected people circulated a chapter draft, an article draft, or some other substantial piece of academic writing. The meeting began with social time (again, this has a great value in and of itself, and I never think of it as "wasted time"). It would then move on to fairly intense and detail-oriented workshopping. This was very useful, but, again, holding regular, timely meetings became a challenge. All members of this group are no longer funded, and so must piece together incomes through multiple low-paying jobs, academic or otherwise. Further, the recent strike of TAs and Course Instructors at the University of Toronto drew all of our time and energy as we fought a bitter battle to raise our income at least a little closer to the poverty line it currently falls shamefully and dramatically short of—as we fought for the first real raise since 2008. The strike was lengthy, bitter, with an intransigent and insulting administration, and its small successes were limited and disheartening. As such, this writing workshop has yet to hold a meeting in 2015, and the future of the group is uncertain. Many of us are badly demoralized. Some are considering dropping out of the program—and these are, I say very earnestly, brilliant scholars who, in a just world, would be the guiding lights of a half dozen English departments a decade hence.

All of these experiences tell me two things. First: there is a great hunger for these groups. They are a locus of hope for senior PhD candidates who are feeling desperate and adrift. Second: these groups are not particularly effective and are often short-lived.

I have some theories as to why both things are so.

Think about a graduate student's training—the upper-year undergraduate seminar, the course-based Master's degree (and it is almost always course-based; at this point, the Master's thesis, where it still exists, is something of an antediluvian survival), the PhD coursework, studying for a set of comprehensive or quali-fying exams. These are all highly structured and hierarchical, but none of them bear resemblance to dissertation writing. My point: graduate students are trained to work well within structures. Graduate school is most accessible to people who thrive in struc-tures. It self-selects for that sort of person—but the institution's hope is that, upon candidacy, the grad student will become a very different kind of person, a person who thrives in a vast open unstructured plane.

I suppose the theory is that, from the moment of candidacy, the aspirant PhD will be self-structuring, having existed within structures for so long. But it's pretty clear: for most of us, when the mould is removed, we slop everywhere, distressingly amorphous; we attempt to attain a structure, but most of us do not have the ability or resources to maintain those attempts. Tightly controlled panic begins to creep in.

The writing or accountability group is one attempt to create and maintain structure. It's an attempt to reintroduce the structure of coursework to the dissertation, to force the blob that is the candidate's life to grow a few bones. A set group of people have regular meetings, with deadlines for producing work; at the meetings, that work is discussed. It certainly looks like a class. But, as Eric Hayot points out in his straightforward and sensible *The Elements of Academic Style*, the practice of professional academic writing bears only a passing resemblance to the kind of writing taught and modeled in graduate courses:

> No one I know writes publishable essays in three weeks, much less when simultaneously working on one or two other essays over the same time period.... The way things work now, a visitor from Mars might reasonably guess that the purpose of the first two or three years of graduate work is to train students in a writing practice designed to generate 75 pages or so over three or four weeks.[1]

As Hayot rightly says, the kind of research and writing experience received up until the moment of candidacy does not train students to a writing practice where months of research lead into

---

1   Eric Hayot, *The Elements of Academic Style: Writing for the Humanities.* (New York and Chichester, West Sussex: Columbia UP, 2014), 10.

months of writing lead into months of revision—where a good, finished, "in the bag" chapter will reasonably take two semesters to complete, if not more.

The structure of the system has set us up to fail—it has taught us to work and write in one way, and then a switch is flipped and we are expected to write and work in a radically different way, one we have had no preparation for, no training in, no familiarity with. Most new candidates don't even have a clear idea of what a dissertation looks like, how it's structured, how it's built. For all our smarts, it's an uncommon graduate student who reads a few dissertations before embarking on the writing of one—and certainly, it's a rarer supervisor or department who suggests such an action to the young PhD. This is partly to do with how the dissertation seems not to matter. It's a bizarre genre, a one-off, neither term paper nor monograph. Once you have written your dissertation, you will never write another dissertation. You only pass once through this particular grinder.

This is one reason why accountability groups fail: they are attempts to reassert the structure of a graduate course, but everyone in the group is fumbling uninformed novice, and, in any case, courses, as we knew and experienced them, are not useful models for dissertation writing, because dissertations are little-understood obscurities.

The other reason these groups fail is also structural. In short: it's the money. Graduate students live a precarious existence well below the poverty line; in order to pay rent and buy groceries, most have to take on extra work, have to piece together a livable income. I can't tell you the number of times an accountability group has melted away because scheduling meetings became impossible due to multiple jobs, academic or not—it's happened twice to me alone.

The solutions to both of these problems seem obvious to me.

First: the training that graduate students receive, prior to candidacy, needs to be retooled so that it inculcates habits and rhythms of professional academic writing. Graduate students need to be familiarized with how a large intellectual project moves from first idea through to finished scholarly monograph. Perhaps, once upon a time, the Master's thesis was useful training in this, but this is no longer the case, as Master's degrees have become pure course work at most institutions.

Without such changes, promoting "writing groups" and "accountability groups" is merely the institution passing its educational responsibility on to the graduate students who are the same students in need of that education. It is like expecting a first year "Great Books" literature survey to be self-taught by the undergraduates who have enrolled in it.

Perhaps PhD coursework needs to be radically reimagined to teach how professional academic writing—public, publishable scholarly writing—is done. Perhaps dissertation writing groups should have faculty shepherds who attend meetings and set or create appropriate structures and goals for the group. Perhaps this is a role that dissertation supervisors can take on—in which case, such duties need to be formally laid out as part of the terms of faculty members' employment.

Another possibility: my department, English, has mandatory Pedagogy and Professionalization classes in the second and fourth years of the PhD, respectively—perhaps a "dissertation writing" class in the third year is in order, where, at the end of the semester, each student will have written a chapter draft through a structure of escalating class assignments (which can then be adapted to the writing of the remaining chapters). Academic writing courses exist, but, at least in the Humanities, at least in my institution, they seem poorly attended. There is a sense (perhaps incorrect) that they teach more basic writing skills to students—primarily in STEM fields—who may be deficient in them. The sense is that they teach the kind of skills a literary scholar, philosopher, or historian mastered quite some time ago. Do any of these classes teach the writing practices of Humanities and Social Sciences professors as they embark on book projects? If not: why not? If so: how can we improve their marketing to reflect their utility to floundering junior scholars in the liberal disciplines, junior scholars who can produce beautiful, grammatical prose without a second thought, but who can't seem to finish that stupid fucking life-ruining chapter draft?

Second: institutional support needs to be radically reimagined. Writing a dissertation is meant to be a full time job. It needs to be paid like one. There is no mystery here. PhD candidates do not have the time and energy to complete dissertations on time because they are distracted by extreme financial and material challenges. I can't stress this enough. We are demoralized and exhausted, like any other employees who are overworked, underpaid, and demonstrably unappreciated by the most powerful within the University (if they actually appreciated us as they claim to do, they would pay us what we're worth). A lost generation of should-be scholars is forming around this problem. Fix it, and dissertations will get written.

Suzanne Conklin Akbari
How I Write

> There is no life in thee, now, except that rocking life imparted by a gentle rolling ship; by her, borrowed from the sea; by the sea, from the inscrutable tides of God. But while this sleep, this dream is on ye, move your foot or hand an inch; slip your hold at all; and your identity comes back in horror. Over Descartian vortices you hover. And perhaps, at midday, in the fairest weather, with one half-throttled shriek you drop through that transparent air into the summer sea, no more to rise for ever.
>
> —Herman Melville, *Moby-Dick*, "The Mast-Head"

Writing is dangerous business. Like the mate keeping watch in the crow's nest, you can spend hours and hours just watching, waiting, hoping for the moment to come when you can at last leap into action. During that long anxious period of waiting, if you're not careful, you may plunge into the "Descartian vortices" below, submerged eternally in the "summer sea." But there is no right way to guard against this danger, no right way to write. This collection of essays, therefore, has as its purpose to describe not how to write, but how we actually do write.

In the initial blog post that unleashed the ensuing landslide of commentary and conversation, Michael Collins argued that doctoral students need better writing support, both in the form of peer communities that provide uncritical support and shared goal-setting, and in the form of structured, scaffolded writing tasks. The first means of support can be facilitated by faculty and administrators, who can provide students with information on building student-led writing groups, good space to work in groups, and so on. The second means of support could also be provided, but would probably have to be provided in the form of supplementary instruction by teachers of writing. The reason: most of us faculty are not equipped to teach writing. Like Alexandra Gillespie, with whom I wrote a joint blog post continuing the conversation launched by Michael, I write in short bursts of productivity that punctuate long periods of frustration and distraction; I don't think that anyone would want to learn to write the way I do. It's possible that faculty who work in a different way, writing a disciplined page or two every morning, could provide the kind of writing mentorship that would be useful to doctoral students. But I have come to think that people simply have different styles of writing: the goal is to figure out what style works for you and learn to do it well.

I know that some faculty do write in a regular, methodical way—a few hundred words every morning, or even a page every day. Such writers include much admired mentors and good friends (some of them appear in these pages). And I have always assumed that my own inability to write in any way other than short bursts of manic activity is pathological. This poses a particular problem in mentoring students as they develop their own writing processes, because I would feel like a complete charlatan telling people to write the way I do: "Procrastinate until you're so consumed with anxiety that you go away and do something else, then let the ideas stew until you're ready to write, then don't talk to anyone for three days while you write. Voilà, article draft!" This is not a sound pedagogical method.

And yet it works. As Alex Gillespie said to me, in the course of one of the Facebook threads arising from Michael Collins's blog post, "Our way is a bit manic but it works right? I mean, we produce. And I enjoy the process." It does indeed work, in the sense that it takes a terribly long time to get ready to write, to come to the point when the trajectory of the argument is clear; but when that time comes, the words pour out. When that time comes, when you're truly in the writing zone, there's nothing like it—it's fantastic, so exhilarating, completely satisfying. I could never get into that frame of mind through daily writing. Which means that it's a form of addiction: the high of writing in a concentrated way, where you no longer think consciously about the words you're writing but just hear the words out loud as you put them on the page, is absolutely intoxicating. So let me summarize a few examples of this experience, what it has felt like to work in this way. I'll begin with an overview of my writing as it developed over the years I spent in graduate school (1988–94); the following several years, as the dissertation evolved into a monograph (1995–2003); and the very different experience of writing a second monograph (2004–08).

When I started writing in graduate school, I was lucky in several ways: 1) I had a remarkable experience of intense training in short-form (three-page) writing, in two graduate seminars on Renaissance poetry; 2) I taught in Columbia's "Logic and Rhetoric" courses, teaching undergraduates to write (and rewrite) frequent short papers; and 3) I stumbled onto a topic in the very first semester of my MA program that would ultimately become the core of my dissertation. While this training in short-form writing—both as student and as teacher—might seem a world away from the long-form dissertation, the rapid turnaround of these short papers gave me the ability to write quickly, without thinking about it too much, as well as good training in close reading practice, both of which became useful building blocks in the dissertation. Teaching this form of writing was just as useful as writing this form, in that it required me to articulate explicitly the stakes of short-form writing in this way, and to guide students through the process.

For this short essay, I'd like to expand a bit on the experience of being trained in short-form writing, something I didn't address in the initial blog post because I thought it had more to do with the topic of teaching than the topic of writing. I've come to think, however, that the two are so deeply intertwined that some discussion of the experience might be worthwhile.

Certainly the experience of writing in those courses did more to shape me as a writer—and as a thinker—than any other experience I had in graduate school. The courses in question went under the deceptively innocent titles of "Seventeenth-century Texts" and "Sixteenth-century English Poetry," taught by Edward Tayler at Columbia University. Tayler was, it must be said, an odd fish, who spoke in a very dry way that was punctuated by moments of utter sincerity. (An evocative description of his teaching style can be found in David Denby's *Great Books*.[1]) He kept a peanut butter jar filled with gin in his desk which he would solemnly bring to the final class meeting, after having told his students, in the penultimate class meeting, to bring mixers.

Tayler was, to say the least, unorthodox, and not just because of the peanut butter jar. He called all of us by our last names, as if we were boys in an English public school (or maybe Andover in the 1950s), and instead of waiting for us to volunteer to speak in class, he would simply ask us to speak. For example, after one student had given a presentation, he might turn to me and say, "Akbari, would you like to disagree with what Vitkus just said?" He had studied each of us carefully enough to know what positions we were likely to take up, and therefore could set us on one another—courteously, politely, with mutual respect—like boxers in the ring. On the way to class on Tuesday evenings (class was always 7–9 P.M.), my heart thudded in my chest as I crossed the quad. I was terrified, but I was also exhilarated, excited about learning, ready for a workout.

All this classroom background is necessary context for the experience of writing for Tayler. In the "Sixteenth-century English Poetry" class, he would assign us to read the entire corpus of one or another poet for each class meeting, and then

---

1   David Denby, *Great Books: My Adventures with Homer, Rousseau, Woolf, and Other Indestructible Writers of the Western World* (New York: Simon and Schuster, 1996), 31-33.

for our assignment, we were to "choose the three best" poems by Wyatt or by Greville and explain the basis for our choices. Choose the "best"? Remember that this was during the period of canon wars and tell me, if you can, what it could possibly mean to choose the "best." The seemingly tone-deaf request was actually an invitation to think about the criteria we bring to literature, the role of conventions (both in the sixteenth century and in the present), and the contingent nature of hierarchy itself. Heady stuff! The exhilaration of the class meetings was mirrored, in an inverted way, by the experience of getting commentary from Tayler on each of the weekly paper assignments. The assignments varied to some extent, week to week, but they were always three-part essays, a maximum of three typed pages. Tayler's commentary was spare to the point of absurdity: he would occasionally underline a word, or add a question mark, or add one of the single-word comments for which he was famous: "More!" "Go!" and, worst of all, "Mebbe." (See below.)

We became eager exegetes, trying to make sense of Tayler's commentary. The experience taught me many things, perhaps most importantly the dynamism and energy that good prose could have. My words on paper could make someone excited, could actually have a kind of motion. Before Tayler, I never imagined that words could feel like that; after Tayler, I can't imagine how I wrote before. As an instructor, while in graduate school at Columbia, I taught the three-part essay in keeping

```
which precede the hundredth emphasize the
ıged imagination whose flaw is the basis of
  5; XCIX 1), literally the inequality or  ̇ℛ, but …
ror essential to the operation of the mind.
self-confusednesses" (11) itself echoes the
  for it seems to be a feminine rhyme with    mebbe
ever, line 11 ends with an extra syllable,
```

with what I had learned from Tayler, and as a faculty member at Toronto, continued to teach the three-part essay in my undergraduate classes—but not in my graduate classes. I couldn't imagine inhabiting the autocratic persona that would be required to put graduate students through the experience I had had in Tayler's classes; besides, the peanut butter jar of gin is, alas, no longer an end-of-term option.

Mastering the three-part essay—first as student, and then as instructor—gave me a high degree of confidence in my ability to write, at least in short forms. I had the opportunity to gain experience with longer-form writing through extended seminar papers, which was a useful (but not transformative) experience. At that time, Columbia MA students were obliged to identify one seminar paper per term as having special status. This paper could be longer than the usual seminar paper, up to about 20 or 22 pages, and would be passed on from the initial instructor to a departmentally appointed second reader. The exercise was a moderately useful one, in that the requirement to think of writing in the longer form (not as long as an article, but longer than a usual seminar paper) asked us to think beyond the usual limits, and to imagine a still longer form of writing that might lie ahead.

In addition to the training in writing that came from Tayler's courses, I benefited enormously from having had the good fortune to find my topic early: in the first term of the MA (in 1988), in a course on Medieval Allegory, I wrote a paper on "The Tripartite Narrator of the First *Roman de la rose*: Dreamer, Lover, and Narcissus." It was a lousy paper, but its preoccupation with visual experience, mythography, and what I would later call "structural allegory" became the core of what became the chapter on Guillaume de Lorris in my dissertation and—ultimately— in the monograph that I published in 2004.

When I started writing the dissertation, I was encouraged—as I still encourage my own students—to begin with the material I knew best. Accordingly, the first chapter I wrote was on the optical allegory of Guillaume's *Rose*. It wasn't a very good dissertation chapter, and it's still the weakest chapter in the book; but it was the very heart of the whole project, the piece from which all the other parts emerged. I can remember sitting in a café in our neighborhood in the early 1990s, thinking about the *Roman de la rose*, reflecting on the two crystals at the bottom of the fountain of Narcissus and the way that white light would be refracted in them. As I thought about the passage, I peered into the surface of the stone in the ring I was wearing, and looked at the different sparks of color that flashed into sight. I felt like I was motionlessly seeing the object of thought; that if I only looked hard enough, I would understand how the parts of the argument related to one another, and I would see the shape of the whole.

In retrospect, that was a self-indulgent and probably silly experience. But it was absolutely central to my writing process. The protracted period of suspension, reading and thinking, doing other things—teaching, looking after children, etc.—were necessary to set the stage for the dissertation writing, which immediately took on a rhythm of its own. I could reliably write one chapter per term, and at the end of three years post-field exams, the dissertation was complete. I cannot emphasize this point often enough: the pace of writing was not because I am a disciplined writer, because I am the opposite of that. But I did have the confidence to believe that the writing would come when it was ready, and I pushed hard to get to the point when the words would be ripe and ready to fall on the page.

The same frustration and sense of deferral marked the years leading up to the ultimate publication of the book that emerged from the dissertation. On the advice of one of my co-supervisors, I put the dissertation aside after the defense. In retrospect, this may not have been good advice, because I found it very difficult to return to this project after a few years, ready to restructure and revise it into monograph form. On the other hand, the length of time that separated dissertation and monograph—nine years—

may have given the work that was ultimately published a greater degree of maturity and cohesiveness would have otherwise been possible. And the tension that existed during that period between the work that I was finishing up (*Seeing Through the Veil*) and the new work that I was developing (what would become *Idols in the East*) was certainly very productive.

Writing a second book was very different from the first, in several ways. The first, and most important difference? I knew that I could write a book, because I had done it; this made it easy to be confident that I could write another one, and the only question was what shape it would take. That shape preoccupied me on and off during the period 1995–2008, most intensely in 2005–07, after publishing *Seeing Through the Veil*, finishing a collection of essays on Marco Polo, and finally turning completely to the task of writing *Idols in the East*. I had initially conceived of the book as separated into chapters focused on individual books or authors—on the model of *Seeing Through the Veil*— but gradually came to think of organizing it thematically, which is a much more difficult shape to control. As with the earlier project, there was a kind of epiphanic experience that came soon before the main part of the writing period: I was walking home, shortly before meeting a friend, and suddenly saw clearly how I wanted to connect the concept of orientation, understood in a polysemous way, to the theory of Orientalism. So I stopped on the street and scribbled some notes on cardinal directions and how identity might be conceived of in spatial terms. That "Aha!" moment was crucial to my writing process. After that moment, it was a matter of shutting myself up in my office, not talking to anyone, eating lunch over my keyboard, and just typing out the words as I heard them.

Again, it sounds pretentious and magical, and completely implausible. But that's what my experience has been like. And it is crucial not to lose sight of the enormous frustration, long periods of the inability to be productive, and painfully acute tendency to be distracted. I spend way more time wanting to write and not finding my way to it than I do in the act of writing. But when it's happening, there's nothing like it.

How can this story be useful to others? Maybe, just maybe, by letting those who are still laboring in the trenches of the dissertation know that there are many different ways of experiencing the creative process—because it is, at least in part, a creative process. Academic writing is basically simple, practical, methodical, steady work; except when it isn't, when it's instead ambitious and exciting and overreaching. I can't imagine having dedicated so much of my life to this work without the rewards of this second aspect of academic writing. So what I would like to say, to those who are now writing their dissertations and feeling frustrated with their own progress, lacking confidence in their abilities to carry out their projects, is: KNOW YOURSELF. Are you able to be a disciplined writer, who puts down a couple of hundred words—or even a whole page—every morning? If so, God bless you, you are one of the lucky ones. That's your process, and it's a remarkably sane and productive one; I often wish I could work in that way.

But if you find yourself thinking about many different things at once—the chapter you should be writing, and the conference abstract that's due next week, and the guest lecture on Ovid you will give next month, and the baby you have to pick up from daycare in a few hours—maybe you simply are that sort of thinker. If so, embrace your process and celebrate it, because you will be able to create the impression of remarkable productivity through the means of what is sometimes called Structured Procrastination. If the chapter isn't coming along, write the conference abstract, even though it's not due for another week; if the abstract isn't coming along, write the lecture that's coming up next month. You procrastinate, avoiding doing the task you should be doing by doing a different task that you also have to do. And the illusion is created—the magnificent illusion—of being able to do a tremendous number of things.

Olivia Beaumont

Alexandra Gillespie
How I Write

I only write when I have to. Because reasons. It's just the way I write.

I used to invent the necessity in "have to." "How will you fund the fourth year of your DPhil?" asked my graduate supervisor in October 1997. I was 23, fresh from an undergraduate degree; I had little Latin, less Greek. (Ha ha! I had no Greek.) I hadn't read much English literature, come to think of it. "I will finish in three years," I told her. "Good," she said.

And because I had said it, I did it. Well, sort of: by October 2000 my thesis existed—not great, but fully footnoted at least.

To get to that point, I needed immediate deadlines as well as deep, energizing anxiety (fear I would not keep my word, fear I would disappoint, fear I would run out of funding). I gave my first year MSt qualifying paper at a conference: high pressure but good fun. After that I scheduled conference presentations for the rest of the thesis. There's nothing like the prospect of giving a paper to "famous" academics to make you write a whole chapter about early printing on the train from Oxford to Glasgow.[1]

Now, by the time I boarded that train, I had seen hundreds of early printed books and I had a database full of notes about them. I had some super OHPTs.[2] I even had some thoughts written down. This is because my advisors would leave fear-

---

1 Early Book Society Conference, July 1999, organized by the lovely Martha Driver and Jeremy Smith.

2 A now defunct technology, remembered fondly by elderly people.

mongering notes in my pigeonhole: "come over for coffee" and such.[3] Terrifying. I would respond defensively, with 5000 words.

But it was the conference-going that was most fruitful. To this day, I do all the writing that really matters to me on the eve of a talk or while I am travelling to deliver it.

Gadding about also gave a productive shape to my academic life. I made friends. I realized how much I needed community. I joined societies, started collaborations, committed to publications, applied for library fellowships, organized a conference, and took on a big load of teaching (my favorite interlocutors are always students).

The end of October 2000 came, and I did have a thesis ready. But somehow I also did not. The argument seemed a bit wrong, and I did not have time to fix it, because I was occupied with all those other "necessities."

So I stalled. I worked on the other stuff for months. Eventually one of my graduate teachers asked the question I was too scared to ask myself: "Alex, when're you gonna hand that thang in?"[4]

Shame is even more productive than fear for me. I went straight home and revised 80,000 words in 19 days. I got about three hours of sleep per night. Towards the end I was so tired that I hallucinated a rat on a can of soup at Sainsbury's. There he was: and then—oh dear! No rat. That was when I decided it really was time to hand the thang in.

None of this was healthy, but it was kind of…great. I had been thinking about problems with my thesis for six months. Solutions emerged in an exuberant rush. I wrote 3000–5000 words a day, including substantial new sections that I later published verbatim in *Print Culture and the Medieval Author* (Oxford, 2006).

---

3   My advisors were Anne Hudson and Helen Cooper, and they were unfailingly generous in every way.

4   Those who know him will recognize the Texan twang of Ralph Hanna III, for whose encouragement I am thankful.

Anyway, that was then. Now I am older (obviously). Various experiences have taught me that fear and anxiety are less necessary to me than I once believed. My professional position is no longer precarious. I have tenure, research funding, brilliant students, glorious colleagues.[5]

But—more accepting, middle aged, and extremely privileged—I still maintain the patterns I established as a graduate student. My time is completely, deliberately filled up. I am up to my teeth in teaching, supervising, grant writing, collaborative project management, commissioned essays, reviews. (I have some principles that guide my selection of activities: (1) Remember the rat! Leave time for sleep. (2) Prioritize kids and partner. (3) Avoid assholes.)

When I can squeeze time out of my schedule, I read and think. I inflict my thoughts on members of my research lab. I visit archives, usually just for a day or two. I scribble ideas down in a notebook. I contribute tl;dr comments to Facebook threads.

And then I write—but only when I have to. A wee while ago, I wrote 6000 words in six hours, so I could send them all to Maura Nolan.[6] This was a lot, even for me. But—Maura Nolan! I'd write 6000 words for Maura any day.

What is to be learned from this? I'm not sure. This essay is very much about me (me, me, me). I offer it mainly because, in a recent Facebook conversation, younger colleagues expressed their belief that all "successful" academics—i.e. the lucky ones with jobs and time to publish—were steady-as-she-goes, 300-words-a-day people. Well, not me.

---

5   Including Suzanne Conklin Akbari, who with Michael Collins, ITM, and my fellow contributors to this book created the space for this discussion.

6   So she could respond to my paper for the Digital Premodern Symposium, May 2014, hosted by Claire Waters and Amanda Phillips, with help from Seeta Chaganti and Colin Milburn. Thanks to them all: I had a blast and got a book chapter out of it!

I suppose my advice about writing is not actually about writing. It's more about "being":

- Learn who you are, and then be that more, instead of thinking, always, that you are meant to be less.

- Be grateful, if you can be.[7]

- Practice patience and empathy with yourself and others. (However, do reserve a little hostility for assholes.[8])

- You are okay, and it will be okay (or else it won't be okay, and that will be okay too).[9] Once you truly believe that, writing and all manner of things will be well.

---

7   I do not say "be grateful" lightly. There are things in my life for which I am far from grateful. But I am grateful for what *is*. I am all good! And so are the people I love. I learned a lot about this (rather to my surprise) from http://thework.com/ (h/t: the wonderful Andrea Bonsey).

8   It is possible to distinguish assholes from people who are just having a little tizzy. Assholes are the ones dumping on people under and around them (but never above them). They seem to be in a lot of pain, but their pain takes an ugly and destructive form. Be empathetic; that will allow you to see that their assholery is not about you. But do not waste your emotional energy on an asshole. And do bear in mind that many of us have internalized others' assholery so completely that we are assholes to our Self, which makes us especially vulnerable to the asshole Other. Some of my colleagues have—flatteringly—compared my own approach to assholes with that of the honey badger (as in https://www.youtube.com/watch?v=4r7wHMg5Yjg). Certainly when it comes to assholes, it is best not to give a single shit.

9   The poet Kate Camp wrote those words down for me on a scrap of paper and gave them to me as farewell gift when I left New Zealand in 1997. I carried it round in my wallet until I finished the DPhil, when I passed it to a friend. But it took me another decade to understand what she meant.

Alice Hutton Sharp
The Community You Have, The Community You Need: On Accountability Groups

For the past two years, two of my graduate school colleagues and I have exchanged daily accountability emails. Sometimes the word "daily" gets a gasp, but indeed: every day (weekends are optional). In the morning, one person sends an email laying out her day's goals and commitments, and the other two chime in as they start their own work. Over the course of the day, someone might shoot out another message, whether a practical question ("Do you guys know how that conference registration website works?"), a complaint ("Why is *x* book not on the library shelf?"), an update ("Email advisor—DONE. Write paragraph—NEXT"), or a victory ("My article was accepted!"). At the end of the day—or the next morning—we each sum up our days. We've used our email to build a virtual office hallway, where we can poke our heads out our doors and express the frustrations, defeats, and triumphs of graduate study. It makes it all less lonely.

The success of our model can be shown by our productivity: we can boast two defended dissertations, and the third member of the group—who started the program a year later—is rapidly progressing on her own writing. A communal CV would also reveal two articles, one postdoc offer, a number of successful conference papers and sessions, and courses taught and TA-ed, as well as other assorted projects in our department and university. We've had one baby, one wedding, and one major surgery, and I think we can say that we suffer no worse mental health than

IMAGE: I promise that the reasons why there was a beer-drinking baby goat at my post-defense party will become clear.

25

your average graduate researcher. We even have social lives and take vacations to see our families or go on camping trips. We still procrastinate. We don't have perfect working methods, and we all have different approaches to how and when we get our work done. The secret is the community.

This was not the first accountability group any of us had tried, and our previous experiences shaped the way we organized our system. We had all participated in once-a-week accountability meetings for our respective doctoral year cohorts, but these fell apart in the face of scheduling and space challenges. Turning to email removed the valuable face-to-face socialization of the weekly coffee meetings, but allowed much more frequent communication. I don't think any of us expected the group to be as durable as it has been, but maximizing flexibility was one key to its success. In addition, the freedom of our accountability group's format means that it can work in conjunction with other groups, whether arranged by an adviser or according to research interest.

Our group was born at the end of a rough day, when I was four months pregnant and had just had a difficult meeting with a committee member about how much work I had left to do. I bought a new notebook and pen to soothe my troubled soul, went home, and drew up an aspirational plan for maximum productivity. (I'm always drawing up aspirational plans for maximum productivity.) I then announced to my husband that I needed someone to keep me accountable to it.

"That's an excellent idea," he said, "and it shouldn't be me." So I emailed two friends, and found that they were in similar ruts with their own research.

Over the course of the evening, we exchanged messages about what form our program should take. I'd first envisioned a scheme in which my friends kept me strictly accountable to my self-improvement plan, like cruel coaches. However, as they both wanted to benefit from the group, but—being sane—had no similar all-encompassing schemes, we decided upon a system of sharing our goals, in which "goals" could be defined however the sender liked. This added reciprocity, strengthening the community we were developing. The purpose of our project was thus to support all three of us, rather than just my own anxiety management. We considered using the chat window in gmail to set goals for individual work sessions, but our times of work productivity did not line up, sending us to a daily model and our email.

This last point was fortuitous, at least for me. I don't think my participation in a work-session model could have survived the whirlwind European research trip I soon took, or the months of intermittent postpartum work. Sometimes we do rely on chat to get through a particularly slow afternoon or draining project, and the immediate support is welcome. We have gotten better at knowing how much work it is reasonable to expect from ourselves in a single day (one of our early hopes for the group), and our community is even stronger than it was before. Regular goal-setting, even without a community, helps you know how much you can achieve for the day and shows you steady progress towards completion; the benefit of the group may not be that it keeps you accountable to your specific plan, but that it keeps you accountable to the process of making a plan.

Starting a Goals Group

In setting up a group, the first question is, of course, choosing your team. I think three people is an ideal number, as it allows for diversity of opinion without being unwieldy (and there's always a backup when someone is traveling). We have found that our friendship is stronger, thanks to our goals group, but that might not be the case if we didn't have compatible personalities and concerns. It is also important that you work with people with whom you can comfortably discuss problems when you aren't getting what you need from the group (more on that below).

If you think your most immediate colleagues will make you more anxious, or more competitive, then my advice is to look further.

You may also want to consider how broad you want the disciplinary spread of your group to be. My group has two literary scholars and me — a historian and manuscript specialist. Sometimes this is a little lonely, as my goals lists look so very different from the others. On the other hand, I never have to worry about feeling competitive about my work.

Another question when setting up such a group — once you have determined your members and your method of communication — is what constitutes a "goal." We interpret it quite broadly: it includes everything from going to the gym (this is never on my list), to wedding planning, to getting the colicky baby to take a nap. This means that our daily achievements reflect the diversity of responsibilities and activities in our lives (always a motivation booster) and helps us keep our academic goals realistic and achievable.

Getting What You Need

It may take a few weeks or months before your working group is running smoothly. While the first messages will likely be full of enthusiasm, you will also need to work out the dynamics of the group and set the boundaries for how much help or advice is to be given. Some people really like to give advice; some people are prone to being pushed around by other peoples' advice. It's important to work with people to whom you can say, "I just want to show you my list for my own accountability, and don't need any advice on it." On the other hand, you may want to ask your peers to keep you honest about the amount of work you can really achieve — particularly if you are prone to managing anxiety by developing unreasonable to-do lists. My group's primary purview is cheerleading: we set goals, sometimes we offer very mild advice on those goals, and when goals are achieved, we celebrate. I would recommend protecting this supportive community by explicitly stating an expectation of confidentiality, such that challenges discussed within the group stay within the group.

Checking Out

Each community has its own customs; ours comes from a misreading. One evening my husband was looking over my shoulder while I sent my evening email, titled "Friday Goals," and thought it read "Friday Goats."

"Hrm," he thought to himself, "they're exchanging pictures of goats."

(Let us consider the fact that he wouldn't have found it surprising if we were.)

As someone who is indeed fond of dairy goats, I recorded the conversation in my email and sent along a picture of a baby Nubian. Now the "Friday Goat" has become our mascot, sent along in celebration when the week is done, and signaling the end of a series of goals.

This leads me to some advice: you should take time away from your work, and the accountability group can be both a help and a hindrance. When you meet once a week for coffee, the meeting eventually comes to an end. Emails rarely do. Not needing to schedule meetings makes the group work for any schedule, but those schedules do not always line up. One member of my group tries to keep her weekends work-free, while I try not to work on Sundays—but true disconnection can be hard when your email is pinging. Much of this is the fault of contemporary communication culture, and not the goals group, but it is something to discuss, and make sure your fellow group members know that there will be times when you are not checking your email. Then turn your phone off, and enjoy your time away.

Although it may sound constraining, however, daily goal check-ins can help you take time away. Reasonable, achievable planning reduces anxiety—you know what you are doing today, and you know that there will be more goals tomorrow (or Monday). Also, because one's time is largely one's own as a graduate student, many people feel like they have to work all the time. When you know your goals for the day, you know when you are done.

Goals and Personalities

There are three types of people who may balk at the suggestion of such a goals group. The first two might find the idea of account-ability too constraining. These people are probably of a sort who like the freedom of working without a plan, or who worry about being embarrassed when they don't achieve their goals. If you truly don't want to set goals for your work, I don't have much advice—except that you reread what I wrote above about know-ing when to stop. For those who worry about failure, I remind you that a perfect score is not the end of the project: the purpose is community and learning how much you can reasonably achieve.

The third type of person may be so devoted to their own personal planning system that they feel they don't need a group. I was one of these for quite some time (remember: aspirational plans for maximum productivity). I still recommend you try a group. (Try a group with people who *do not want your advice.*) Things will happen, and your plans will fail. It's better to have encouragement when they do than to try to be self-sufficient. My accountability group offered unfailing support as I struggled with the disconnect between what I could do and what I wanted to get done after my son was born. I rarely (well, only some-times) draw up aspirational and ultimately unachievable plans for productivity anymore. Paradoxically, having a goals group has actually made me much more flexible, as well as more productive.

Goal: Writing

This is how I experienced it: when we began our group I was four months pregnant, coming up on the sixth year of my doctoral program, and still digging my way through the manuscripts that would make up the bulk of my dissertation. I was weighed down by an immense amount of anxiety around the Latin texts, much of which will be familiar to anyone who has done a graduate degree. There was so much work to be done, and what if I wasn't smart enough to do it? I procrastinated. I dithered. I felt like an imposter. I tried to write a full chapter on the text with minimal discussion of textual variants; my adviser hated it. (Justly.) In the first months of our goals groups, my lists were text-oriented: *Transcribe three folios of x manuscript*, I wrote. *Collate two folios of y.* When I went to Europe, the manuscripts came to the fore, but I continued to work on my transcriptions and began writing a chapter based on the manuscript descriptions: *See Amiens manuscript and write description.* Slowly and steadily the bulk of my research, and my first chapter, grew—goal by goal.

My parents are writers, and I have always been a writer. I have been a daily writer. I have been a binge writer. I have been a blocked, anxious, terrified (and burnt-out) writer. I have been a passionate, absorbed, sleeping-with-the-laptop-to-work-first-thing writer, and having experienced that exhilaration keeps me going through dry spells. I would prefer to be a daily writer, but my-life-as-lived makes this a challenge to achieve. My current writing methods are influenced by my experience working with medieval texts. I complete small, discrete writing tasks daily, for binges of varying length—a week, a fortnight, a month, a summer. On Easter Monday of 2014, I decided to finish a rough draft of my dissertation by the feast of its most important subject, Saint Augustine (August 28th). Writing momentum built on itself so that in the end, I submitted the first week of September. (I could have finished earlier, perhaps, if I had spent less time on the Excel spreadsheet on which I tracked my word-count goals and their relationship to reality.)

By learning how to break my project into small, achievable pieces through both my transcription work and the goals group, I learned how to break a long-format academic work into manageable stages. The techniques I use are many and varied—loose journaling about an academic problem for fifteen to twenty minutes, sketching out visual maps of my argument, outlining, drafting the "shitty first draft" that Anne Lamott has made famous. Writing goals is itself a stage of writing, and listing my intermediate tasks to the goals group gives them a weight and legitimacy they might otherwise lack. In discussing my writing progress with friends, I've learned new techniques and I have developed a good sense of how much time I will need for each task, allowing me to schedule realistic binges of daily writing.

I have always been a writer. But for many years of writing I depended on perfect conditions: an immaculate desk, the privacy of an empty room—or lacking these, the panic of procrastination and the loneliness of an all-nighter. When I gave up my desk to make room for a crib, I panicked. Would I ever finish? Would I resent my baby? (My own mother, writing an essay like this one, had complained of losing her office to make my nursery.[1]) With the goals group, I have written on trains, I have written in Tim Horton's surrounded by flirting pre-teens, I have written at the dining room table. I write this now on the porch of a relative's home, with my group awaiting news of a completed goal. What I needed was not perfect circumstances—what I needed was community.

---

1   Frances Phillips, "Allowance: A Poetics of Motherhood," in *The Grand Permission: New Writings on Poetics and Motherhood*, edited by Patricia Dienstfrey and Brenda Hillman (Middleton, CT: Wesleyan University Press, 2003), 171–176.

Franks Casket

spectacular whalebone casket
probably made in the Anglo-Saxon
dom of Northumbria. Modelled on
Christian caskets, it was most likely
ed in a monastery for a significant
haps royal – patron. The casket's
ry, accompanied by runic and Latin
tions, comes from an array of
s including Germanic and Roman
s, the Bible, and historical events.

Asa Simon Mittman
This Would Be Better
If I Had a Co-Author

This would be better if I had a co-author. Of *course* it would. This would mean a few things (ideally, and assuming that all went according to plan):

– We'd have had a conversation before starting to write, before outlining, about what the essay should look like, how it should be framed and organized, and what it might accomplish. As is, I've just had that conversation bouncing around in my head while trying to fall asleep for the last few nights. I think best in dialog, often only articulating for myself what I want to say when I try to explain it to someone else. Collaborative writing is a sustained conversation.

– Starting (again, this is my ideal scenario) with the first few pages—written by me, or by my imagined co-author—the essay would have a second set of eyes on it. We might use a shared Google Doc, and write simultaneously, watching one another's words appear as if from the ghost in the machine, but that's varsity-level collaboration, probably not to be tried the first time out. Here, my first round of feedback will come at the end, when the essay is already as long as need be, already framed and organized and written, and only then sent in to Suzanne Akbari. By then, substantive changes are so very hard. All the connective tissue, all the sinew must be torn apart to make even minor changes. From the start, while building, everything is easy.

35

– A co-author would necessitate that I fight my own impulses as a writer. This is a good thing for me, and I suspect it is for most writers. More below.

– Finally, and most importantly, I'd be *thinking differently* from the start, trying to think not only as and for myself, but also trying to think through and about the interests and concerns of my co-author, trying not to merely write "my half" of an essay, but to write a whole, in parts.

Like most academics in the humanities, I was trained in graduate school—really, in all of the schools I attended from kindergarten on through my PhD—to be a solitary writer. I was told to do my own work, to write my own essays, that "unauthorized collaboration" was an academic violation. In college and graduate school, I was never asked or assigned to write with a classmate, and I'm pretty sure, at that point, that I would not have wanted to. I was trained to (figuratively) head up to my lonely garret, where I'd find (in the cinematic retelling, with me played by George Clooney) a manual typewriter and a glass of scotch, and where, in the middle of the night, in furious bursts of energy, I'd hammer out my own (brilliant! genius!) ideas, inscribing and asserting my identity with every clattering keystroke. This Romantic nineteenth-century model of authorship still obtains in the early twenty-first, and I think it is high time to abandon it. There are some movements afoot to press toward more collaboration, including the Material Collective's encouragement of co-written conference papers and publications. I don't want to mandate this for everyone, of course, and collaboration is not the right path for every project. However, I'd like to see collaborative work become the guiding assumption and industry standard, rather than an unusual deviation from the solitary norm. In the last decade or so, I've been actively seeking out writing partners, and have co-written pieces of varied length (blog post to book) with about a dozen colleagues. Each one is better than what I'd have written on the subject, writing alone. *This piece*, too, would surely be better with a co-author.

How I Write When Writing Solo

If I am to write a piece without a collaborator, I generally revert to my training. I conceive an idea, read as much as I have time to, outline—at times, in obsessive detail, though working with some co-authors has gotten me to loosen up some in this regard—and then I write. I start at the introduction, write the body, and then add on a conclusion, generally writing in that orderly order. I add all my notes and apparatus as I write. It is all quite dull and unfit for cinematic portrayal. I compose pretty quickly, and generally (more or less) enjoy the process. My writing mantra is "fifteen minutes *is* enough time to get something written." (Actually, we just finished an episode of *Dr. Who*, and while my wife is brushing her teeth, I've added a few lines, here. Plenty of time to accomplish something, especially since this essay is only sup-posed to be 2500–3000 words.) I don't have a "zone," never work late, and have never pulled an all-nighter, even in college. For me, writing is generally not a fraught exercise, not filled with angst or anxiety except as regards meeting deadlines, which I firmly believe in doing, *every time*.

I pace and drive my writing by committing to conference talks and other such speaking gigs. If I have agreed to speak for fifteen or forty-five minutes on a subject, I'd better have the requisite number of pages drafted and in reasonable shape by then. I also obsess over my images for talks, so that means I've got to have the thing written enough in advance to spend a few (several) hours polishing up my Keynote or Prezi (though half the time, the screen turns out to be tiny and crooked, or the projector dim, or the lighting in the room too bright for anyone to really appreciate the care). Most of what I've written, then, was written in ten-page bursts, in advance of Kalamazoo, Medieval Association of the Pacific, Leeds, New Chaucer Society, and so on. Of course, these are collaborative venues; the reason we come together is because we are seeking to get and give help, though the suggestions and corrections and support we receive at conferences usually goes uncredited. (Yes, I know, I know, not everyone is constructive and helpful, and there is a lot of grandstanding and sniping and other such foolishness, but if that was all there was, we'd stop going. That's just something we put up with to get the good stuff, and should work to discourage in a number of ways.)

When writing solo, I do have one perhaps wasteful practice. I am by nature somewhat contrarian, and I enjoy a good intellectual debate. In essence, that's what the whole scholarly enterprise is, or at least might be. I am often, implicitly or explicitly writing *against* something or someone, which again, is part of our training: find a flaw in previous scholarship and correct it, or find a gap and fill it. This is the stance with which most dissertations begin. My first-draft introductions tend to be obnoxious, belittling, and self-aggrandizing. "Look at how stupid all past scholarship has been! Look at how smart *I* am, in comparison!" I find writing such introductions to be very useful. They help me organize my thinking on a subject, systemize my understanding of the historiography, and give me a (usually straw man) opponent to fight as I write, which animates the process and gives the rest of my writing a bit more zip. But thankfully the wonderful Suzanne Lewis, my graduate school advisor, taught me to always, in the end, *cut these sections*. They remain a common part of my writing process, but I don't publish them. They may be helpful, but they are also foolish and petty and deeply ungenerous. Should I have told you about writing them, at all? I promise that I've never done this with something *you* wrote. I love your writing. Oy vey, I wish I'd discussed all of this with someone before starting. Am I getting somewhere? Is this making sense? I have no idea. Surely, this would be better organized, and better written, if I had a co-author.

What (I Think) I Am Like as a Collaborator

Great! Prompt! Reasonable! Supportive! Patient! Oh, and *very* needy. I am a needy collaborator. I want to talk *a lot*. I might email you four times in a given day. Or five (half-joking subject lines read, for example, "Message 6 of 9 Today!"). And I'll want to hear back from you often. I'll worry about the deadline, and will really, really want to get our draft in by then, if not a bit before. I'll want time to write and pass the essay to you, to think while you write and pass it back to me, and so on. It will be my guiding hope that we are doing more than each writing two separate halves and then stitching them together at the end. I want to write a cohesive piece that neither of us could have written on our own, not only because of disciplinary and subject area specialties but also because of personalities and writing voices and individual concerns. I want to be pressed and stretched.

Oh, and if you like, especially if you aren't an art historian, I'll offer to deal with the headache of permissions, and with putting together the final image files and whatnot. Of course, if you *are* an art historian (or other image-y person) and are willing to take half the stack of permissions requests, *thank you!* It really is the worst part of the writing process. Or I'll make you a deal: I'll do the permissions if you will proof the notes. That is even worse.

All of this collaboration is a lot of work. I suspect that I've written as many words in emails to my collaborators as in my writings with them. In the humanities, in my experience, hiring committees, tenure and promotion committees, and administrators often see collaborative writing as a lesser activity, and co-written pieces as soft additions to a CV. I once interviewed for a job listed as seeking a medieval art historian with a specialty in "interdisciplinary collaboration." I thought I was perfect for it. In the interview, the chair of the committee asked me what I was working on. I spoke for a few minutes about my then-current collaborative, interdisciplinary book (*Inconceivable Beasts: The Wonders of the East in the* Beowulf *Manuscript*, co-authored with my long-term writing partner and dear friend, Susan Kim). The committee looked demonstratively bored, so I paused, and the second I did, the chair pointedly leaped in to ask, "What is your next *solo* project?" But in the ad you asked…Never mind. Thankfully, my colleagues at Chico are happy with my approach to publishing and other work, so this is no longer a concern, but it was quite apparent in my years on the job market.

There seems to be some sort of assumption that co-writing is easier and faster, is some sort of cheating. I was asked about the same project, in a different job interview, "Which half of the book did you write?" Which half? I wrote the whole bloody thing! *As did Susan Kim.* That's what collaboration ideally is, as I see it. I stand by every word in the book, even (especially?) if I can spot, here and there, phrases that are characteristic of Susan's writing, or ideas characteristic of her thought processes.

Part of signing on for a collaboration—maybe the most important and difficult part—is allowing another person to inhabit my words. I have a pretty strong voice, speaking and writing (shocking admission, I know). Friends have said that when they read my writing, they can't help but hear me speaking the text in their heads. (Sorry about that, everyone.) It is a great act of trust and recognition to say, "Here are my words, my thoughts, my concerns and preoccupations. Do what you like with them." I care passionately about the subjects on which I write. Why else do it? I'm tenured, and don't get any particular reward at my university for publishing, at this point (though I am well-supported and feel appreciated). I write about what I want to write about, on the schedule I choose (though I really need to learn to say yes to fewer projects). The ability to choose my own intellectual life, only fettered by my own abilities, creativity, and the time I've got in which to work, is a fabulous luxury. But it is even better when I've got a co-author's abilities, creativity, and time, as well. Having this would certainly improve this little piece.

How Collaborating Goes, in Practice

I wish I could say that every collaboration I've had has been equally fulfilling and rewarding, but of course, like all human relationships, they vary quite a bit. Some have been just ideal— intellectually rich and exciting and full of interchange, and resulting in work that is not merely better than what I could do on my own but also profoundly *different* from what I would have done. On the other hand, a couple of my planned collaborations just didn't happen; they fell apart at one stage or another. In some cases, the project just went away. In others, I carried on unaccompanied, since the piece was promised somewhere. They turned out fine, but I think they'd have been better with their intended co-authors.

Some collaborations, of course, have been in the middle. The work got done (more or less on time), the process was interesting, and not too frustrating, and I'm happy with the results. I am very glad to say that I've not yet (knock on wood) lost a friend over a collaboration. I've heard from a few colleagues that they have, and some of these have sworn off collaborative work, but to me, this seems like giving up on dating because of a bad relationship. A bad experience doesn't negate the value of the enterprise. I want to tell these folks to get back in the game! Plenty of other fish in the sea!

I think I've figured out what the trouble has been in those cases where things have been somewhat challenging. Like most relationship problems, it comes down to a lack of open communication. I plan to start all future collaborations with a conversation about what I am like to write with (at least as far as I know), and to ask my potential co-authors to fess up, too. If I *know* that your process is to vanish for a week or two, here and there, and you agree to say that you are falling off the grid for a fortnight, fine, I can manage. If I don't know this, I'll panic. I think that Michael Collins started a great conversation, and that Suzanne has done something wonderful in putting together this collection, which I hope will inspire more such statements about writing, formal and informal. They would be a great place to start to get a sense of what might be in store.

When co-writing, in practice, in most cases, I think I probably generate more draft words than my co-authors, because I am verbose and my writing starts out somewhat chattily. I love adjectives and adverbs, and think that runs of them can be quite delightful. I've only found one co-author so far, I think, who is quite as loquacious as I am. That was an essay that got written *very* quickly, and was tremendous fun. But in general, I am appreciative of the more ruminative pace of other co-authors. They force me to slow down my writing, which means more thinking and rethinking. They also notice when I am using rhetoric to cover for lack of clarity in my thinking, or simply because I am enjoying the sound of my own authorial voice, regardless of whether or not it aids the discussion. I agree with James Elkins's account of writing:

> Much of art history…is not entirely conscious…Thinking about art and history is, I think, is like daydreaming: we drift in and out of awareness of what we're doing. Sometimes it may be clear what impels me to write a certain passage; other days, I have very little idea why a certain theory rings true, or a certain phrase sounds right.[1]

1   James Elkins, *Our Beautiful, Dry, and Distant Texts: Art History as Writing* (University Park, PA: Penn State Press, 1997), xx.

ASA SIMON MITTMAN

For all of my careful planning and outlining, I often get off-script and down various rabbit holes and country lanes (mixing metaphors with wild abandon), and they are not always good routes to take. Waiting for a reply once I've sent a batch off to a co-author gives me time and space to think through my strategies. Why did I write that? *Should* I have written that? If I am writing solo, I generally just keep on going, and the first feedback I get will likely be at a conference, after I've given a piece of what is probably already a larger chapter that has therefore become much harder to edit than it would have been when it was three or five pages. A few paragraphs in, everything is as soft and malleable as wax. It is simple and painless to move, shift, transform, or delete. This is rather less the case when a chapter is written.

Our general working model in the humanities is to write in isolation—several friends actually set up writing retreats or drop offline or engage in other such quarantining practices, and I get it! It is hard to focus when the computer keeps pinging us to say that we have new messages and posts and all that. It is worth it to me, though, for the human contact, for the extended exchange on subjects of mutual interest. These conversations might last for the space of a blog post, or for a decade and counting.

To my collaborators and co-authors, past, present, and future, then, thank you for your great generosity in allowing me to inhabit your words, to dig into your ideas, to borrow your knowledge, and to share in your play with the wonderful objects, texts, and themes that drew us to work together in the first place. Thank you for shooting for grants with me (and sharing the rewards), for traveling and co-speaking and sitting side-by-side in gob-smacked awe of a thing that has managed to survive a thousand years, only to end up, for a day, in our tremulous hands. Thank you for thinking with me, and for replying to *all* my damned emails. I probably should have gotten one or two or ten of you to write this with me. It would be better if I had.

Jeffrey Jerome Cohen
On the Necessity of Ignoring Those Who Offer Themselves as Examples

Habit and Routine (A Blog Post, 2011)

Two versions of the same aphorism seem equally true: "Habit and routine are the nemeses of innovation" and "Habit and routine are the precondition of innovation." When it comes to writing, I need a familiar time, schedule and space…and I need to break out of this regularity sometimes since it offers the ingredients not only for accomplishment but boredom. I finished my doctoral program from start to finish in a fairly quick five years (having entered directly from undergraduate) in part because I did not stall at the writing stage. Funding and being miserable helped, but so did routine and a semester of teaching release. Each morning I would bike a wide circuit through Cambridge, along the Charles River via the Esplanade, and over to Newbury Street. There I'd sit with my books at a coffee shop. With a refillable mug and a slice of marble pound cake, I would pore over whatever writing I'd accomplished the previous day, filling the printout with marginalia (this was long before laptops were affordable). I'd then add as much as possible to what I had just revised, attempting to extend the chapter as far as I could. When fatigue eventually set in, I'd turn to a book or essay I'd brought along. Back on my bike around lunchtime, home to eat quickly (yogurt, banana, granola: always the same), and then at my computer, typing in whatever changes I'd made and transcribing the new paragraphs I'd penned.

This daily routine of bike rides and writing in two locations sustained me through the most intense period of composing my thesis. Biking was an essential part of my thinking, not a delay. Most of my research was already done, so I didn't need to visit the library often. I also had drafted thorough outlines of how I expected chapters to unwind. Even if each was in the end disobedient, possessing a road map for each was essential to writing without agonizing over what comes next. During my final semester in graduate school, I was assigned to TA two different classes, Shakespeare and History of English. Time for bike rides evaporated, but the reshuffling of my schedule wasn't a complete catastrophe. I invented some new routines, and managed to carve smaller spaces within which to write intensely, helped along by a firm deadline for submission and a passion to be done. Work, I learned, has a way of filling all available space.

I don't want to idealize this period. Days were solitary to the point (at times) of sadness. Often I'd throw away what I had written as a false start or a dead end. But I kept at it. Throughout graduate school I also lived with at least one person, and found a powerful motivation in knowing that if I worked as hard as I could during the day I might not have to spend a night locked in my room with a computer and a hundred open books. And I suppose that also shows another reason I could get the writing done: I am rewards-driven as well as generally too impatient to procrastinate. I hate having my post-deadline time robbed by a project that overspills its allotted frame, even when the deadline is self-imposed.

Ever since children entered the picture my working days are significantly shorter than those I describe above. When Katherine and Alex are home, I don't want to be cloistered in the study. I try to end my writing just before they arrive, except for email and odds and ends. It doesn't always work and chaos (in the form of sick days and snow days) enters the equation frequently. Possessing a comfortable space dedicated to writing is essential: the former nursery of our house, a room about the size of a walk-in closet into which I've somehow managed to fit all my important books.

Other strategies that I use, with varying degrees of success:

– Every day I wake up at 5 AM and (on most of them) run. That seems crazy, I know, but holds many rewards. The world is more vivid at that liminal hour. Running provides me with solitude and reflection to start the day, and I feel better afterwards.

– I try to write or revise *something* every morning. My mind shuts off late in the afternoon so I cannot do much more than email.

– Sometimes I simply can't get the words out of me. I fiddle with what I've written, I surf the internet, I go back and try again. But if writing doesn't come it doesn't come. I let myself off the hook rather than allow self-recrimination to snowball. Sometimes you need a fallow day to obtain a fertile one.

– I reward myself with small amounts of social media after writing for a bit. Reading blogs or Facebook doesn't neces-sarily distract from getting work accomplished; sometimes it is the small break needed to return with more focus.

– I use an outline not only for my writing, but for my time. I focus on getting a semi-discrete task accomplished within a time period—a particular section of an essay written, a cer-tain book read. I use Google Calendar and Apple Remind-ers to keep track of approaching deadlines and portion out my time. I try not to miss these deadlines because then I screw up the work schedule. I have too much travel and too many essays due to allow that to happen without triggering panic.

– In writing all this down I realize that one of the reasons these strategies work for me is that I'm disciplined—as well as, I admit, relentless to the point of being annoying, even to myself. I've sometimes not been a good collaborator because of my calendaring and my drive. These strategies likely won't work for many because they would be oppressive rather than liberating.

– Conference papers (and other public talks) are great motivators because, well, who wants to commit an Epic Fail for an audience?

– Running, practicing guitar, swimming with the kids, cooking dinner, having lunch with a friend and off-topic reading are not distractions from my writing. They are what enable me to approach it with freshness and, when it is working well, without resentment. I have to remind myself of this fact repeatedly.

– Writing can be immensely pleasurable. I love it when I get a sentence right, or when a text opens as it never has before, or the argument I am formulating suddenly seems to *work*. But writing can also be agony, or just tedious. The only way out is a focus on a long view and small joys, because they alone will carry you through.

Writing Lockdown
(Some Facebook Status Updates, 2013)

DAY 1

Writing Lockdown begins now, fifty summer days committed to long hours spent on nothing but the manuscript of *Stone: An Ecology of the Inhuman*. I watched *The Shining* last night to prepare.

DAY 3

Made progress reworking introduction to be less chirpy. Started on first chapter, a recursive monster of a thing. First bout of project induced melancholia—or maybe it's the usual early summer funk. Progress will continue tomorrow at an undisclosed location due to fact son will be home practicing "like a thousand times" the song for the final exam in his piano class.

DAY 4

Have discovered that revising is as enjoyable as poking sticks in your eye again and again. Imagined I was Bartleby, but the version who can't stop typing away at a book chapter even when his eyes hurt from all the poking. Ate a ginger cookie in Bartleby's honor.

DAY 10

The cashier at the Undisclosed Location where I try to do an hour of writing lockdown each morning insisted that my coffee is on the house because I'm now a regular.

DAY 11

Encountered much of my writing at its worst (sentences that run on so long they leave their subjects stranded twenty lines from their verbs, catalogs so lengthy they gesture towards infinity, repetitions that tend towards redundancy), but also accomplished some rigorous thinking about the ultimate shape of the book. I do have confidence that it will come together, in time. I've sketched out three possibilities for its final form and we will see what clarity tomorrow brings. Unlike last Friday, when I was declaring that an untimely death would at least free me of this albatross, today I lack lucidity about the final shape of the thing but it seems OK.

DAY 13

Today did not start well, mostly due to insomnia about Writing Lockdown and the shitty chapter I am faced with revising.

DAY 17

No matter how long I looked at the chapter most words seemed ill chosen and the argument I thought I had nailed down dis-

persed into chains of associative logic and topical meandering.
I have a string of terms I can't make cohere and the whole thing
seems a repetitious amalgam that doesn't accomplish much (and
yet is the product of a great deal of research and labor). The chapter kicked my butt. I need to, um, sit on a pillow or something so
that it doesn't do that to me again.

DAY 19
A half day: Wendy and I will escape to Luray for a long weekend,
where exploring some caves and hiking the mountains will keep
the geologic real even when lockdown is suspended. I feel OK
about departing the hermitage because yesterday's deadlock was
broken by an outpouring of helpful FB comments (44!) as I tried
to wrap my mind around rocks and terminological failure. All hail
the power of social media—and the generosity of those who use it.

DAY 20
After an awesome Geologic Shenandoah Escape, Writing
Lockdown began inauspiciously last night with a massive onset
of anxiety matched with the thunderous nearing of a storm: each
reverberating boom was a footstep of Day 20 approaching and
the topple back into my book. Threaten as it did, however, the
storm never arrived, and after a tense hour I fell asleep…and
maybe that is a sign that return to lockdown will be OK.

DAY 21
Still going strong. 12 hours after waking up this morning,
chapter now seems vastly improved in a critical section. If,
however, I am ever compelled to write anything at any point
ever again in my career about medieval carbuncles, O FOOL,
I SHALL GO MAD.

DAY 24

The turgidity of my prose depresses me enough that today I retrench a bit, pruning and clarifying rather than attempting to finish. Puts me off schedule but I'm thinking of it as a cleaning day, just as sometimes the only way to get work done at your desk is to diminish the clutter.

DAY 26

Book chapter down to 25K words, but an incoherent mess that shows no sign of wanting to organize itself into unity. Not a great day.

DAY 28

My reserves of creativity are tapped out, and my chapter is an embarrassment to rational beings everywhere. AND the copy-edited manuscript of *Prismatic Ecology* just arrived. And Wendy is having surgery on her hand tomorrow.

DAY 29

Rather than post an update that mewls about my insomnia, the flooding storms, the work I have to accomplish, Wendy's surgery and the things to do beforehand, I will simply note that (1) Writing Lockdown Day 29 will be a soporific half day; (2) I know that I am very fortunate to have a life that allows me to devote time to writing and rewards me for what I've undertaken, (3) much of that good life comes about from the support of family, good friends, and you, the person reading this: I'm grateful for your companionship.

DAY 32

The end of Writing Lockdown Day 32 witnesses my body rebelling against this regime. My shoulders smart, my right wrist is sore from the edge of the laptop pressing into it, the arch of my

left foot aches from the crazy position I place it when I'm not
paying attention.

DAY 35

Blue clouds against black sky, and the radiant Thunder Moon
behind. A good omen from this morning's run for Writing
Lockdown.

DAY 40

40 days and 40 nights of Writing Lockdown either means
I'm Noah sailing in an ark full of chapters which are in turn
crammed with horrendously strained metaphors OR that I have
only two weeks of Writing Lockdown remaining before depar-
ture for Maine.

DAY 41

Writing Lockdown Day 41 ends with the drawing of a necessary
line. I could read endlessly and add infinite amounts of material to this book but I need to stop somewhere…and this is my
somewhere. Now I start the process of going through the book
slowly and carefully to ensure the writing is up to snuff, the argument fully coheres, the footnotes are worked out, and everything
is mechanically perfect.

DAY 42

I wish Douglas Adams were still alive so that he could tell me
what Writing Lockdown Day 42 means.

DAY 46

Frustrating day. Tried so hard to complete revision of chapter;
failed. Discovered that closing section also appears verbatim in
last chapter. Overall structure not gelling. Too many quotes, too

much digression. Tomorrow had better yield an epiphany or I will complain or Facebook or something.

DAY 48

A reminder of the affective roller coaster intense writing projects produce. After the happiness of yesterday's small achievement, a night of a single, short, dull and infinitely looping dream that kept waking me up—agitated by its inane repetition, and angry enough at my brain that I'd stay awake for an hour. Reset. Repeat. Anxiety, because Writing Lockdown is nearly over.

DAY 49

Thinking about the health costs of this long regimen. Losing the 75 lbs might be possible but the curvature of my spine and the heroin addiction are going to be more difficult to address.

DAY 50

Writing Lockdown began on June 3 and has repeated intensely fifty times. I've been working like a dog. But even summer dog days come to their close, and mine terminate now. Writing Lockdown ends NOW with a Dark n Stormy.

Backwards Glance
(written on a holiday when I got up early due to stress over having too much writing to do, 2015)

I composed the words that appear above on social media: the blog In the Middle (www.inthemedievalmiddle.com) and Facebook (www.facebook.com/jjcohen). The blog post records a time in my life when I was good at getting things done. I wish that time had lasted longer. By the summer of 2013 I had taken on so many projects—and had a book due to press—that I was plagued by insomnia and constantly anxious that I would not be able to complete all that loomed. I used fifty nonsequential days that summer as a Writing Lockdown, working harder than ever so that I could get *Stone* ready for press. My plan was to have the manuscript almost there by the second week of August so that I could enjoy a family vacation hiking in Acadia without bringing books or thinking academic thoughts. I posted about the

Lockdown every day on Facebook as a way of being accountable to the world outside my mind. Reading through these posts now I can see that there will come day when my relentless drive will cause me harm.

Well, honestly, it *did* cause me harm: I was something of a wreck by the end of the process, emotionally and physically. I injured my shoulder badly enough that it took several months of physical therapy to restore full function. People think the life of the mind is not dangerous, but it will kill you, if you let it. If I could travel back in time I would tell the Jeffrey Cohen of graduate school, 2011, and 2013 to *chill the hell out*. I offer these words and reflections here knowing full well that underneath the processes I describe run currents of apprehensiveness, fear, self-punishing discipline, and relentless drive that I do not think is healthy and is certainly not offered for emulation. What I want to say in closing is that no one can tell you how to write, only how she or he writes. That process changes as life proceeds: writing is a mode of living, and must therefore be adaptable. Possibilities exist within every model. And so do perils.

Maura Nolan
How I Write

I direct a campus-wide program called Berkeley Connect that began in the English Department, in which advanced graduate students mentor undergraduates one-on-one and in groups to create a small-college experience at our large research university. In any given semester, we have a number of public events for participants that focus on bringing faculty, graduate students, and undergraduates closer together, as people engaged in the same enterprise at different levels. One of our most successful events is a panel we have done several times, called "How I Write." We ask five department faculty and graduate students to speak for ten minutes each about their writing practices—not how to be better writers, or how to organize papers, or how to come up with a thesis, or how to do research, but what they actually do when they sit down at their computers or desks with a blank screen or page in front of them. Students love hearing about the crazy things their mentors and professors do to make themselves write. One graduate student reported tying himself to his desk chair with his bathrobe belt so he couldn't get up and walk around. Others had elaborate systems for keeping score of words, paragraphs, pages, footnotes, and chapters written, with rewards for each type of accomplishment. What means the most to students, however—and what is the biggest revelation to them—is the fact that these experts on English literature all *struggle* with writing. As teachers, none of us had realized the extent to which our undergraduates assumed that being an English graduate student or an English professor, and thus a proven success at literary criticism, meant that writing must be very easy for you. The correlate to this assumption, of course,

IMAGE: Faintly written on the card: "Dear Maura, I hope you get well. I hope your tooth feels beter. Love, Siobhan."

59

is that if you are struggling with writing, *that must mean you aren't very good at it*. Our students simply hadn't understood that good writing is the product of a difficult process; that the process doesn't necessarily get easier as your skill increases; that writing one book (or two or three) doesn't make the next one a walk in the park; and that good writing always means re-writing. It was clear that they thought we sat down at our computers, started a book with the first word of the introduction, wrote fluidly and quickly for three hundred pages, and typed THE END, probably while drinking a gin and tonic. No revision necessary.

Hearing a distinguished Berkeley professor, the author of multiple books, explain that he struggled every time he sat down to write transformed the idea of writing for our undergraduate listeners. They stopped thinking that their struggles were indices of their inadequacy. Or at least, we gave them a bulwark against that thought. As we all know, writing is a practice that sparks incredible creativity in the part of the brain that is responsible for self-criticism and self-loathing. These panels were good for us, too. The graduate mentors, who were all at various stages of dissertation writing, left the discussion incredibly energized by hearing about writing practices from their peers and their professors. Those of us on the faculty left with a new understanding of how important it is to demystify the process of academic writing, to strip away the mythology that has shrouded professors in such mystery that students have assumed we write with ease.

That isn't to say that writing isn't a lot easier than it once was, for me at least. But I would describe the difference between my past experience and present experience as "having learned the rudiments of a skill" rather than as "having refined a skill I already had." Of course I knew how to write when I started my dissertation. So do most students. But they aren't academic writers, nor was I. I didn't learn how to be an academic writer until I started publishing, getting readers' reports, and sharing my work with mentors. Being a "writer of seminar papers" or a "writer of conference papers" or a "writer of book reviews" or a blogger or a tweeter is not the same as being the kind of academic writer that finishing a dissertation—and working with a dissertation advisor—teaches you to be.

In *Writing Degree Zero*, Roland Barthes claimed that the writer fundamentally does not know herself, that she writes according to a style that she cannot dissect or predict, that is at the same time unique and distinctive to her.[1] Understanding this combination of distinctiveness and alienation is critically important to mentoring academic writers, particularly as they begin their dissertations. I always tell my PhD students that writing a dissertation is one of the most intense exercises in self-knowledge that one can undertake. Almost none of the writing students do before the dissertation prepares them for this intensity, which they often experience as a new sense of being scrutinized. A bright white light seems to be shining on them and their writing, an unflattering light that reveals every mistake, every typo, every sophomoric play on words, making even the best turns of phrase sound juvenile. This vivid sense of being looked at comes from the dissertation's status as one of the first public documents that most students write; it is their official entry into academia as credentialed speakers and it is thus subject to community judgment in a way that course papers, blog entries, Twitter posts, and other kinds of writing are not. The writer's awareness of this community gaze, which is embodied in the person of the dissertation director, is part of what makes writing a dissertation so painful.

This account—in which the writer wilts under the surveillance of the disciplinary structure of the institution—is a rather

---

1   Roland Barthes, *Writing Degree Zero*, trans. Annette Lavers and Colin Smith (New York: Hill and Wang, 1967), 10–12.

Foucauldian description of dissertation writing that betrays my early 90s graduate education. We were all convinced we were under surveillance at the time, along with everyone we wrote about; it was an era when Power reigned supreme, but always in such deceitful, secretive ways that it required literary critics to expose its subtle workings. A lot of what got said in the name of Foucault was just silly, of course, just as always happens when a powerful body of thought is iterated and reiterated at greater and greater distances from its original context. But some Foucauldian insights struck a terrible truth in our hearts. The idea that we were entering a public arena as dissertation writers, an arena in which we would be subject to the judgmental gaze of our chosen community, was one of them. And I don't think, despite the invention of the Internet and the new level of comfort many students feel with public writing, that that truth about the dissertation has changed very much. Indeed, given the fact that your dissertation is now effectively published online, unless you are able to embargo it (which is not a given, as many are finding out), the intensity of the community gaze upon the dissertation has increased exponentially. In my day, if you were unhappy with your dissertation, you could always seek out the library copy, move it somewhere in the library where it would never be found (perhaps in the TG416 classification, where the books about "steel plate deck bridges" are shelved), tuck it in behind some large old books, and rest assured that no one would ever find it. Of course, some enterprising soul could always order the microfilm, but almost no one ever did that. Now dissertations are a couple of clicks away. If my generation felt that writing a dissertation created a sense of exposure, current dissertators must feel like someone replaced the hundred-watt bulb in the spotlight with a 500-watt halogen torch.

At this stage in my life, I see this process from the perspective of a dissertation advisor, someone who is helping students manage that sense of exposure by developing a style that is sturdy enough to carry them through an entire career of public writing. In one sense, that means that I embody the community gaze, the gaze of judgment: that is why students are often surprised to find that their first chapter draft elicits much more commentary from me than a course paper. They are surprised because they haven't made the mental adjustment necessary to writing a dissertation: they haven't begun to imagine that their audience goes beyond the comfortable one-to-one dyad of teacher and student. My job is to embody that larger audience and the kind of pressure that it will eventually put on the student's work, in the form of reader's reports, press reports, book reviews, and the like. I've spent many years reading articles and book manuscripts for journals and presses, and I have often been struck by the degree to which some young authors seem oblivious to community standards. In those cases, I tend to feel that it is the dissertation director's responsibility to teach—and insist on—those community standards in order to prepare her student for the exercise of community judgment. That is step one in the formation of an academic style: submitting oneself to the norms of the discursive community one wishes to join.

Step two in this process centers on an ongoing dialogue between advisor and student about the student's writing. I have already quoted Barthes on style as something opaque to the writer, something about herself that she does not know. What I haven't said is that such a state of affairs is all well and good if the writer is fully developed, an expert at her craft; her own opacities recede in importance as her style becomes more and more successful. But becoming a better writer means knowing something about your own writing—your habits, your tics, your turns of phrase, your weak spots, your strengths. You can't change what you don't recognize in yourself. The person who teaches students about themselves as writers is their dissertation advisor. In the dark wood of the student's style, the advisor becomes a kind of Virgil to the student's Dante, showing her how she writes now and pointing the way to a better way of writing in the future. Let's say, for example, that the student habitually writes sentences in which the subject and the verb are miles apart, so far apart that her sentences are hard to understand. The problem is that the writer herself has no trouble understanding her sentences. For her, the words on the page don't act like signifiers. They act like mnemonic devices. They might as well be runes, or emojis, or binary code. All they do is trigger a memory of what she was thinking when she wrote the sentence. So when she reads it, she doesn't think about what the words mean or where they are placed or how they interact with each other; her eyes see the shapes and the memory is instantly sparked and she thinks, "that sentence is crystal-clear." In contrast, the advisor reads every word as if she had never seen it before, presuming nothing about what the student intends, waiting to see what meaning the sentence—as it is written—will generate. The advisor has no memory of the original thought. So when the subject appears, and the verb is nowhere to be found, and lots and lots of words interfere and obfuscate, the advisor notices that subject-verb separation is a writing habit.

This example is very small. There are many more complex examples I could describe, but they all boil down to the same gap between the writer's tendency to treat her writing as an opaque sign whose meaning is supplied by memory and the advisor's method of reading, in which the words on the page are interpreted as given, in their full multivalence and with the full semantic complexity of a reader's expectations for English prose in mind. The course of writing a dissertation is in part a process of learning how to adopt that interpretive method of reading for oneself—to read one's own work as if it had been written by a stranger. But the learning curve is inevitably asymptotic. No one, as Barthes knew, can see herself whole. That is why our profession is so deeply rooted in peer review. It isn't because the profession is hierarchical and requires gatekeepers to reinforce its hierarchy. It is because most writers can't read their own writing very well. Since they can't do that, they can't become better writers on their own. And while it may not matter very much that a given writer improves a particular article or writes a better book about Middle English, I think it is of exceeding importance that the quality of writing in Middle English scholarship (or Old English, or Early Modern, or Eighteenth-century scholarship) be constantly improving. Our writing as a collective body should get better all the time. A robust peer review system is the only way to make that happen, because getting reader's reports from people who don't know you or your background or your intentions is the best possible way to judge what your words have actually communicated to a reader.

They aren't always pleasant. I've gotten some that were really miserable to read, because what I was arguing hit the reader the wrong way. One threw up his hands after a long list of my failings and said, "I completely disagree with this reading of Lydgate, but I can see that this is the trend of the future, so I won't stand in its way." I have to say, however, that once I put my offended pride aside and really looked at his critiques, I could see that what had happened was that I had failed to properly communicate my argument. What he disagreed with was a version of my argument that was not what I had intended to convey. I revised. The revised version still wasn't a version that this particular reader would have liked; nothing, short of turning my Lydgate into his Lydgate, would have done that. But at least if he and I were to disagree in print, he would be responding to the claims I actually wanted to make—not the claims that I had seemed to make by virtue of ambiguous wording and careless juxtapositions. His hostility and doubt made him a really good reader, someone who would find my points of weakness, notice when I was papering over the cracks, and always choose the least flattering interpretation of an ambiguous point. What made him a great reader was that he also acknowledged his bias: opinions about Lydgate had undergone a titanic shift in his lifetime and he recognized that the consensus of the field was an important factor in making judgments about publication.

How I Write

In response to the blog posts that inspired this collection, I commented that writing habits change over the course of a life-time, citing disability and family as two possible reasons. I don't have children, so my writing has never had to accommodate the demands of an infant, a toddler, a young child, a preteen, or a teenager. But I do have friends, and my friends have children, and I'm the oldest of five children. So I'm very familiar with the fundamentally inimical nature of child-rearing to writing, if you conceive of writing as something that has to happen in a quiet, clean, well-ordered, private place. A room of one's own, in fact. Some people can never give up this ideal and reserve writing for their office at school, or for the very early morning, or late at night. But from my observation, the most successful people are the ones who treat writing as a practice they can shoehorn into any time or space, no matter how small. A correlative to this observation is that these bits of time have to be given over to writing, rather than doing the million other things that a working parent could find to do with twenty extra minutes. Load the dishwasher or write a paragraph? Fold the laundry or copyedit a few pages? Work on your article while sitting in the bleachers at soccer practice or read graduate applications for the committee meeting next week? I used to think that only some people have the kinds of brains that can pick up and put down their writing all day long like this. But then I developed an urgent need to find more time in the day for writing and I learned that, as with so many other aspects of the brain, neuroplasticity can work wonders.

Ten years ago, I was diagnosed with MS.[2] The resulting disability has changed the way I write dramatically. As a graduate student, it took me some time to learn that the only effective way for me to work was to write every day, early in the morning, with a set goal, far in advance of any deadline. Deadlines had a terrible effect on me. Unlike some people, I did not rise to the occasion of a deadline. I would postpone writing something, thinking "there's plenty of time," until the deadline was imminent. Then I would sit down, assess what had to be done, face the fact that doing it would take an incredible outlay of effort, and be gripped by an anxiety so intense that I simply stopped. Total paralysis was my response to impending deadlines, just as avoidance was my response to far-away deadlines. The solution was simple: move the day of reckoning, the day when I assessed what had to be done for a particular project, back by a couple of months (for an article) or years (for a book). Armed with an accurate assessment of what I had to do, I could calmly write a reasonable amount every day and finish with time to revise before the deadline. That is what I did.

I wrote my first book very early in the morning, with the goal of writing one thousand words every day. I included footnotes in this tally. As soon as I had written one thousand words, the anxiety receded. At that point, I could write more. I could go to the library and do research. I could spend the rest of the day reading. As long as I was adding up units of one thousand words every day, I was making reasonable progress toward finishing the project in time to go up for tenure. This method worked for me for a long time.

---

2   The picture that accompanies this essay was drawn for me by my niece, Siobhan Dale (age 7), when I was first diagnosed in 2004 with chronic facial pain and the dental pain that goes with it. A small percentage of MS patients present with facial pain as the first symptom of the illness; it was several more years before my MS was diagnosed. The picture has hung over my desk ever since, cheering me on with its invincible optimism about my teeth.

Of course, it worked best when I was on leave. But it fitted nicely into an academic day as well, because I was finished with my writing stint before I had to leave for work. In retrospect, I think one of the reasons I liked it was because it controlled the amount of writing I did in a day, fencing it off in the morning and leaving the rest of the day free. I wouldn't have understood that at the time, because I still thought I had to force myself to write. But as time has gone on, and the demands on my time have increased, writing has become a dangerous lure away from other projects; I start doing it, and four hours later, I realize I have a memo due tomorrow, proposals to read, emails to write, and it's midnight. It's much the most enjoyable thing I have to do and it's addictive; I want to do it all the time, when I should be doing other things.

What my disability has meant is that I can no longer work in the early mornings. Fatigue is also a serious obstacle to long stretches of work. I have nerve damage in my right wrist and hand, which prevents me from typing, so I now dictate everything using voice recognition software. Above all, as I think anyone with a disabling chronic disease will confirm, I have lost the ability to predict what any given day will be like. When I wrote my book, every day was the same. I knew I could get up at 5:00 and work; I knew I could go running at 10:00; I knew fairly accurately how I would feel most days. Chronic illness is not predictable. You never know what day will be a good day and what day will be a bad day; when you will be able to get up early and when you will need an extra hour of sleep. Life becomes a game of playing the odds—you make appointments at times when you are usually at your best; you set your teaching time for the good part of the day; you build extra time into conference travel, in case you need a day to recover from the plane trip. How does writing fit into this scenario? For one thing, I've stopped fearing deadlines. Or rather, I no longer have the luxury of peacefully writing essays a little bit at a time months in advance. Instead, I fit them in wherever I can. I come home from work and spend the evening at my computer if I have an essay to write, because that's the only time I can find for writing. My TV-viewing has really suffered. I carry my faithful iPad wherever I go, because I often find stolen hours during the day for writing. I depend on a research assistant for help with getting books from the library and scanning articles and documents that I need, because I can no longer stand for long periods or carry heavy loads. Every day is a series of readjustments that depends on the variable of my health, which is remarkably unpredictable. One might think that a good night's sleep, regular exercise, and eating well would produce a "good day" and overtiredness and eating toast for dinner would result in an unproductive tomorrow. One would think that. Often enough, however, good behavior produces bad results and bad behavior produces—not good results, but okay results. That's in the short term, of course; in the long term, taking care of yourself matters. But it doesn't necessarily allow you to have a good writing day on demand.

There are three important things that having a disability teaches you, all of which are relevant to writing. First, everyone you know will eventually have a disability. It's part of aging. I have more in common with my parents than I have with my peers in relation to physical health; we have many of the same challenges and symptoms. Every accommodation that you receive or that you insist upon at your university is an accommodation that some of your peers will eventually need as they age. Of course, many of them will be retired by then. But enough of them will still be working that those accommodations will make it possible for them to keep writing, too.

Second, when you have a disability, any illusions you might have had about self-reliance are shown the door. There are things you can't do; you need other people to do them for you. But you realize at the same time that your previous sense of self-reliance was a false one; even when you were healthy, you existed in a web of dependencies and mutual support. The disabled person may indeed need physical help, but offers in return other kinds of intellectual, emotional, and moral support to his or her community. The writing that seems so solitary when you are sitting at your computer is in fact one node in a network of connections on which all academics rely. To return to an earlier part of this essay, that is why peer review is such a critical part of our enterprise. We have to challenge each other to be better; we have to model good writing for novices in our community; we have to be willing to submit to critique. At the same time, as readers, we have to exercise wise judgment. We have to know the difference between what we don't like and what isn't very good, between an argument with which we disagree and a bad argument.

What achieving wise judgment requires is humility, the humility that acknowledges an essay is good enough for publication even if it makes an argument you hate, the humility that admits that a negative reader's report makes valid points about your writing. And the last thing I will mention that having a disability teaches you is humility. It is humbling to ask other people for help. It is humbling to be unable to meet a deadline, or to bow out of a conference. It is humbling to admit that the demands of the body supersede the will. But with humility comes compassion and openness to change, a willingness to listen to others on their own terms and the flexibility to adapt to new circumstances. When the Wife of Bath's hag lectures her new husband about gentility, poverty, and age, she comments that:

> Poverte ful ofte, whan a man is lowe,
> Maketh his God and eek hymself to knowe.
> Poverte a spectacle is, as thynketh me,
> Thurgh which he may his verray freendes see.[3]
>
> (III: 1201–1204)

---

3   *The Riverside Chaucer*, ed. Larry D. Benson (Boston: Houghton Mifflin, 1987).

I commented earlier that writing a dissertation is an experience of coming to know yourself as a writer; our profession, more than almost any other, demands a rigorous exercise of self-knowledge as part of its credentialing process. True to the hag's pronouncement, that exercise includes an extended period of poverty, otherwise known as graduate education. Disability, like poverty, like dissertation-writing, brings about a reassessment. You put on new spectacles and see new things—new relationships between people, new causes, new injustices, a new landscape (where are the accessible elevators? Where are the curb cuts? Can I sit in an aisle seat?). That new vision doesn't have to be as bleak as the hag's prediction, which seems to suggest that false friends will abound. But it will be different. I am fortunate to be a professor and a literary critic, because having a life as a writer means that however different the physical landscape looks around me—and whatever technologies I have to use to continue writing—the writing remains to be done. Chaucer isn't going away. If I were a doctor or a lawyer or an electrician, I might not be able to do my job. But writing is something you can do even when you can't do very much else. Like love, it is a "craft so long to lerne"—but unlike courtly love, it is a craft that won't desert you.[4]

4   Chaucer, *The Parliament of Fowls*, line 1.

Richard H. Godden
Errant Practices

I don't know how.
I don't know how to write.
I don't know how to write well.

These words were painful to write. They haunt me, and have done so my entire academic career. Ok, that is not entirely true. I made it through my first two years of college on pure bluster, but once I needed to *write*, to do more than toss off a handful of pages in a single night, I became haunted. I spent most of the second half of college and, frankly, all of my graduate career feeling like I had skipped a year of schooling. I had gone away, I know not where, and when I came back, everyone was doing long division and I was scrambling to figure out what I missed. Why was I never taught how to write properly? Why did I never learn? Why do I struggle so much?

* * *

I remember one particularly painful incident. I had just had a meeting about my first chapter of my dissertation. It...did not go well. It was all wrong, and my advisor was quite blunt about it. Looking back over those early pages, he was quite right. He gave me some advice on how to fix it, but I can't remember it now. What I remember is pacing in front of the library for about an hour. I must have made a somewhat comic spectacle, a guy in a wheelchair literally driving in circles. I've always been a pacer, peripatetic in my wanderings. For someone who has chosen a career marked by its sedentary nature, I am restless. I also remember being darkly amused that I was physically enacting my mental state—I was stuck in a circuit, and going nowhere.

During my elliptical journey, someone stopped me to ask what I was doing. (Incidentally, it is somehow outrageously funny to some people that I pace.) Not quite in the mood to talk, I mentioned briefly that I was a graduate student, and that I was writing in my head. I should mention that this was during the summer, and my interlocutor was one of many people attending a writing institute on campus. For the next five minutes, despite my best efforts to disentangle myself from the conversation, this person began to tell me, with the zeal of someone just having glimpsed the Eleusinian mysteries, that what I needed to do was *just write*. Sit down, and do it. Stop putting it off. Get thee to a desk and *write*. This, apparently, was the secret.

I've heard this many times. Just do it. It is a sheer act of will. On a more helpful note, I have also heard advice according to what I like to call "the Runner's Guide to Writing"—write *x* amount of words a day, or write during a certain time of day, every day. For example, I've been told about waking up and sitting down to one's desk every day, at 8 A.M., and writing for a set amount of time. Or, the writer will not stop until they have written 500, 1000, or 2000 words. A variation of this would be the Pomodoro Technique, where you write for short, distraction-free bursts (25–35 minutes), scheduling several throughout the day, spaced out to preserve energy and focus. I deeply admire (and envy) the people that can commit to such disciplined schedules. I've tried to do this well over a dozen times, yet I have failed each time. Part of my failure might be due to my somewhat restless nature, but a significant part of it is simply that this system does not work for me. As someone with a physical disability, I often have difficulty gauging what a given day for me will be like. Will I feel well? Will I encounter any difficulties with such simple things like using the restroom or gaining access to food and caffeine? As a result, I constantly end up breaking whatever rhythm

I might have developed over a short span of days, and inevitably, at least until recently, I have always borne such interruption as a personal mark of failure.

But despite my frustrations, I find myself constantly seeking new methods or rituals. I use the word "ritual" quite intentionally here as many people seem to have one. Many employ certain kinds of music, or inhabit particular environments, or cultivate a specific order for doing things. No matter how much we try to make the practice of writing transparent, it remains mystified. It does to me, and I know I am not alone in this.

Every few weeks, I see a fellow academic on Twitter or Facebook asking for advice about how to simply *write*. At that point, loads of people share their experiences—the best feedback is often framed as "what works for me," but occasionally you get a devout practitioner of some method or another. Other recurring pieces of advice involve regular exercise, working in particular or varying spaces, or the adoption of something like a standing desk. Invariably I find many of these pieces of advice useful, but there are many that I simply cannot follow. For obvious reasons, I am not going to be someone to use a standing desk. However, even changing locations can be difficult for me. Increasingly, I find myself using a dictation program for about 50% of my writing. I do so because dictation helps alleviate some of the physical difficulties I have with typing for long periods of time, which is fantastic, but also a bit difficult to do in public spaces. So, while my favorite coffee shop might rejuvenate me intellectually, there would be consequences in terms of the actual amount of writing I could get done.

So far, I am only writing about writing in a negative way. "What you do does not work for me." I do not mean this to be accusatory, or self-pitying. Rather, I am relating some of this because I deeply believe that I am not alone. Yes, my experiences are perhaps cast into a sharper relief because of physical limitations, but we all struggle with this. I've spoken to so many people who have expressed some sense that they write *differently* or *wrong*. I have encountered this quite a bit from academic colleagues, both junior and senior, graduate students and tenured faculty. There is often nervous laughter, or false bluster, or pained looks followed by staring off into the distance. Yes, not everyone struggles like this, but enough do that I do not think anyone should feel embarrassed about it. Or ashamed. (I am embarrassed. And ashamed.)

* * *

When I was approached to compose this piece for this particular volume, I was encouraged to think about the intersections between my own experience writing and my experience teaching writing. Like many people who earned their PhDs in the last six or seven years, I have taught quite a bit of composition, at a few different institutions. Over the years, I have certainly developed my own particular approach to teaching writing at the University level, but it is only with composing this piece that I have really put together some of the ways that my own experience has shaped my pedagogy.

On the very first day of class, I tell my students that the goal of the course is not to make them write like I do—the goal of the course is to help them "become the best possible version of themselves as writers" that they can be, at this time. Initially, this likely comes off as an empty platitude, but this notion guides everything that I do in the classroom. I work to help my students figure out what strategies work for them, and what don't. I emphasize the notion of strategy over rule. If it works, it works.

Every semester, I hear from a statistically significant number of my students that they have been told, or simply have learned from experience, that they cannot write well. Every semester. Every section. These ideas have become so internalized for these students that many of them simply accept it as the way things are. I also encounter resistance and anxiety when I suggest new habits or practices, such as beginning to write before having a fully formulated thesis, or using the first-person singular in their writing. Not all, but many of my students carry with them various rules about what can or cannot be done in writing. These rules are often treated as something holy. One student once described to me how a teacher had codified several rules into what students cheekily called, "The Executioner's Block." We all had a good laugh at this, and almost all were willing to test or leave behind some of the rules they had been taught. But, they would all seem to be looking over their shoulder while doing so. The specter of English teachers past might come into the room at any moment.

So that I am not misunderstood, I want to state unequivocally that I am not mocking or ridiculing high school writing instruction. Sometimes we do need these rules to learn. On a deeper level, however, I think that many writers crave these rules. We want to know the secret. We want to know how to get things done. We want to know how to write well. But, I consistently refuse to share any such secrets with my students, if only because I myself am not privy to such revelations. The only truth I've learned about writing is that there is no singular prescription, even though we all yearn for one.

Increasingly, I practice in my class what is known as *inclusive pedagogy*. An inclusive pedagogy accepts the idea that we all learn differently, and that we all use learning tools differently. Instead of creating normative rules and practices (which then include various exceptions), I try to avoid the binaries of normal/exception and disabled/normal in favor of encouraging and cultivating choice for all learning and writing styles.

Here is one example that keeps being a topic in higher education periodicals and social media: the use of laptops and other devices in class. A growing critical consensus is being reached that technology in the classroom distracts too much, and that students learn much better when they take notes by hand. So, over the past year or two there have been repeated articles about the benefits of banning screens in the classroom. Aside from the fact that this is a policy I could not abide by as my handwriting is both laborious and illegible, this desire to ban certain forms of technology partially arises from the sense that there is a *best* way to learn. This is the best method, science has proven it, and so all students must conform.

However, those embracing technology bans often acknowledge that accommodations or exceptions must be made for the disabled (including here physical and learning disability). While I have seen students become quite distracted by their devices, I remain committed to the idea that some students learn better with them. I give them the opportunity to figure out what works or doesn't for their own needs. For instance, I've seen quite a few second-language learners use their phone as a quick dictionary, and I've heard from various students that they do better in some classes when typing notes, but for other courses they prefer to handwrite. These are, of course, anecdotal reports that I have gotten from my own class, but the larger point that I'm trying to make is that we all learn differently. We all write differently.

Beyond note-taking, what does this mean for the classroom? It means I encourage more experimentation, and I talk openly about the idea of failure. Sometimes we try something and it simply does not work. Sometimes it does. I have a colleague at my University who is currently experimenting with more flexible deadlines, giving students a week to turn in major assignments as opposed to a solid and sometimes punishing deadline. I have not yet done this in my own course, but I think it might be the next step in an inclusive pedagogical classroom.

While my students want me to demystify the writing process, I am working, instead, to personalize it for them. I want them to move past the idea that there is one right way to do it, because all too often that leads to the feeling that they are doing it wrong. I know this because I share that feeling. I still throw out ideas, even rituals, and I especially share strategies, but I try not to make any of them prescriptive. Whether intentional or not, too much writing advice often comes across as normative, which can be not only ableist, but also alienating for so many. So, in my struggle to find a writing process that works for me both in terms of temperament and physical ability, I have found myself adopting an inclusive pedagogy, even when I did not have the vocabulary to frame my approach in terms of disability or normative practice. When you find something that works for you, that can be a wondrous thing, but do not assume it will work for anyone else.

* * *

Okay, so how do I write? To be honest, I still do not know.

I know that my writing style is changing as I use dictation more and type less (I hope this creates a more accessible style as opposed to obscure academic prose). I know that I don't write as often as I would like, especially when I spend a long day on campus teaching and therefore I have neither the space, nor the tools available for me to write. I know that I do a lot of writing in my head. When I was younger, and still studying math, I would often be frustrated at the need to "show one's work" because I would do most of the steps in my head, and then record the answer. I did not do this because I was lazy, but because handwriting was difficult. Those early strategies have stayed with me—I tend to write in short bursts when my head has become too full, and I feel like I'm about to burst. I (try) to give myself permission to wander, to delay, and even to fail.

I use any technology available to me. Frankly, my dissertation would never have been finished were it not for Google Books and similar services that allowed me to quickly search for the quotations that I needed—too many times I would remember that I needed something from a book, only to have it high up on a shelf and out of my reach for several hours. I have become skilled in the art of Google-fu.

I accept that some days do not include writing. Sometimes several days will go by and I will not have written anything. Am I lazy? Undisciplined? To some, it might seem like it. But, I do not know any other way to do it. I do not know how to write well. But I hope it happens anyway.

na diſtingueret

nc alieno. Et e

ia hnc aliua f

teuãd. egacquí

n conſ regm nn

cepta cont foꝛm

ad que dapñ

Bruce Holsinger
Cushion, Kernel, Craft

How do I write? At the moment, writing this, I'm stretched out on a green leather couch, laptop on a thin pillow, rescue mutt at my feet. I write half the time while reclined on this couch, the other half while slouched in various coffee shops around town, or hunched in plastic chairs at airport gates. I haven't written meaningful prose while sitting at a desk since graduate school. Desks are props for student meetings, email composition, and the production of administrative verbiage. When I write creatively, whether fiction or criticism, I'm sprawled horizontally with my bare feet on a cushion or a coffee table, or else I'm drooped over my MacBook at a café counter. I thrive on noise, distraction, pets, people. Lots of coffee.

And variety. Over the last several years I've learned quite a lot about my academic writing (and my academic writing habits) through the lens of my newer vocation as a novelist. It's taken a few stumbling attempts to figure out a good and healthy balance between fiction and criticism—though this balance has less to do with time than with disposition. When producing fiction I'm generally in a state of enthralment, losing myself for hours at a stretch and experiencing the act of writing as pure joy. Even if I'm composing a research-heavy chapter in a historical novel, or working through a line-by-line revision of a scene of dialogue, I'm nearly always taking pleasure in the task (some would call this "flow," I suppose).

Academic writing represents an entirely different experience for me. Sentences don't come easily; they never have. Even when I'm producing a good number of words a day I often find the work of literary analysis or theoretical argument a source of screaming frustration. This frustration shows on the page, which tends to be an ugly mess until the very late draft stages in any given piece of writing. My physical disposition while writing mirrors the in-progress state of my academic prose. It's okay to be sloppy, I constantly reassure myself. You don't have to be organized, systematic, sequential, off-line, ponderous, or even grammatical, and correct punctuation is purely optional. If you saw what my in-progress documents look like in their early stages you would understand how central disorganization, mess, and sprawl are to my "process," such as it is.

Don't believe me? I think I can illustrate what I'm talking about with a simple visual aid. So I know pretty much what I'm going to say (or rather, what I'm *going to have said*) in those two preceding paragraphs. But they're not written yet, let alone polished. I've decided on the spot to finish *this* paragraph first to help make a point. Now I'll take a screen shot of those two preceding paragraphs in their current state and put a box around them. Okay, done. Now I'll paste that screenshot into this paragraph. Done. Here's what those last two paragraphs look like at this very moment:

> Writing fiction: I've learned an awful lot about my academic writing ?. new vocation as a fiction writer, , taken a while and some stumbling attempts to figure out ?. utter joy, lose myself for hours or days at a time UGH , and otherwise making shit up. Academic writing is entirely different. But fiction has helped me gain a much-needed distance on my academic writing and ? its purpose, its idiom, its . ?. Here I'll say just a few words about the ?. fuckfuckfuckfuckfuck
>
> The physical disposition ?. maps onto ?. First, I've always told myself, it's okay to be sloppy. You don't have to be organized, systematic, alphabetical, sequential, off-line, ponderous, or . , If you saw one of my disorganized notes, . ? fiction .

The sentence you're reading now is the last sentence of the current paragraph, which is as complete and as polished as it's going to get.

Notice how random and scattered these unformed paragraphs in the screenshot are (were) at this (that) point. No complete sentences, few coherent thoughts, some self-castigation, even some swearing. Yet the seeds of everything in the final versions of these paragraphs are already apparent in the gobbledygook that eventually (over about a week of on-and-off drafting and refining) produced them. And this exercise is helping me identify something else about my writing. I tend to structure my work-in-progress paragraph by paragraph, indents and all, even if the initial content of those paragraphs is mostly gibberish, expressionist punctuation, and half-formed ruminations. The paragraph can be a very helpful unit of thought and written expression to think with and work with. Though I'm not an outliner, I'll often block out a piece a few paragraphs at a time, asking myself what each paragraph needs to accomplish within the course of my argument.

The same holds true for chapters within books. I write books as single Microsoft Word documents, never creating separate docs for chapters or sections, and I'm rarely working on only one chapter or section at at time. Nor do I write chapters (let alone books) from beginning to end. I tend to begin somewhere in the indeterminate middle. I've always been in awe and maybe slightly suspicious of people who can write fiction or criticism in polished sentences from start to finish.

* * *

Producing a book is for me, then, a process of slow but impatient and inevitably disordered accretion, though I would also emphasize the importance of inductive reasoning and inductive writing: starting from the smallest thing, the fragment, and working outward and upward to larger conclusions and statements of argument. When I'm writing about literature or about a theoretical work, I nearly always start with a passage from a literary text or other primary source I'm thinking about in that moment.

When I say "begin with," I mean that literally: I begin by simply typing into a blank document the stanza, the few lines of poetry, the couple of sentences that are in that moment sparking my interest. Then I stare at them for a while. Then I'll check Facebook, send an email, walk the dog. Then I'll stare at them again. I'll type twenty words, delete them, swear quietly a number of times, itch a mosquito bite, worry at a hangnail, check Facebook again, post something. I'll go recycle a jar. Wipe down a counter. Return to my couch.

And then, finally, I'll say something about the words in front of me. The first thing I write will be quite simple and usually descriptive: an observation about a metaphor in the passage, a comment on the rhymed words in a stanza or alliterated words in a line, a question about a tangly or provocative formulation that could use some lexical picking apart, a paraphrase of a snippet of theory. Often these initial bursts of prose will come in the form of notes to myself rather than coherent or well-formulated thoughts, though once I'm at this stage I've truly begun the process that will someday be recognizable as critical writing. Often it's those first sentences I type that contain the eventual core of my argument.

The same point came home to me in a different way when I taught our department's dissertation seminar a few years ago. This two-semester course is designed for students in the PhD program who are in the process of writing the dissertation prospectus, that seven-to-ten-page bundle of lies and futility. One of the most frequent anxieties I heard from graduate students preparing to enroll in the seminar was the fear of the blank page (or the blinking cursor). How do I begin a huge project like this from scratch? What do I actually *put* on that page, and how should I start?

Wanting to be helpful but also specific, I went back and looked through the last four or five book chapters or articles I'd written, then thought for a while about how exactly I wrote them, trying to reconstruct where, in what order, and with what specific sentences they had begun. I realized they nearly all had one thing in common: they began in a specific moment of engagement with a small (usually literary) detail typed up and sitting in front of me *before* I started writing about it.

So I created a first assignment for the seminar that would encourage the students to experiment with just such an initial fragment, a little something to write about, write with, write around—"the kernel," I called it. Here is the assignment, exactly as I distributed it in diss sem. I'm including it here not to be prescriptive, but rather to illustrate what I've come to understand is my process of working up from the small detail into a more generalizing analytical mode.

Assignment 1: The Kernel

The goal of this first assignment of our calendar year together is to get you writing actual pages that will eventually show up in your dissertation, and perhaps your prospectus. Academic writing can and should be a process of discovery. It will be in and through your writing over the next several years that you will generate the founding ideas and interpretive ingenuities that will form your intellectual and professional identity in the years ahead. But this process of discovery begins and ends with the objects before us: primarily, in our discipline's case, the literary artifacts that command our sustained reflection and engagement over the course of many pages and many years.

To that end, we'll begin with a deceptively straightforward assignment. I want you to identify for me what you see at this moment as the kernel of your prospective dissertation: that line, stanza, poem, sentence, paragraph, chapter, metaphor, image, physical object, or abstraction that most intrigues you, or puzzles you, or moves you, or repulses you into considering it worthy of your sustained critical attention.

To put this another way, if you had to start writing your dissertation tomorrow, what would be your founding text or object, and with what particular fragment of it would you begin? Your kernel might be a snippet of dialogue from *Titus Andronicus*, an anonymous lyric preserved in a fifteenth-century manuscript, an illustration by Blake, a confounding paragraph from *Mrs. Dalloway* or *Cane* or *Finnegans Wake*, or an ephemeral snippet of experimental digital poetry. If you feel you're not quite at the point where you can settle on one object or fragment, risk it anyway: the stakes of this assignment are low, and you can complete it simply by writing about a line or passage that speaks in some way to your current interests, however unformed.

Once you have identified your kernel, I want you to think about it for a while and then just start writing. Describe it, summarize it, and contextualize it for me briefly; then, most importantly, interpret it. Let its complexity, its provocation, guide your analysis as you explore what about this kernel most intrigues you. Pay attention, if you're so inclined, to form and style—rhetoric, syntax, diction, rhythm, prosody—so that your initial interpretation speaks to the literary

substance of your object rather than simply its historical or political theme. The only real stipulation here is
that your pages may not derive from a seminar paper
or any other previously written work. They need to be
fresh writing that thinks anew about what's in front of
you. No need for footnotes or references of any kind.
If you want to engage in dialogue with another critic
or two that's fine, but citations aren't necessary.

I would like you to write 3–5 pages, double-spaced,
to hand in at some point before our next meeting,
which will take place Friday, February 24, at 9:30. I will
respond and meet with you individually to discuss this
assignment by the end of February. You should complete this more inductive assignment while you work on
Assignment 2: Comparative Dissertation Report, which
will be presented orally in seminar that day.

This sort of practical, in-the-moment approach to beginning
essays, chapters, and books has always helped me get going even
if my thoughts are hopelessly jumbled and I have no earthly
idea what I'm going to be arguing in the pages ahead. It gets
words on the page, and that can sometimes be the most important thing. Let's say your goal is to write five hundred words of
your book or your dissertation every day. Some days you'll write
more, some less, but five hundred words will usually make you
feel good about your progress. Well, if you simply type into your
document two stanzas of Chaucer's rhyme royal, you've already
produced twenty percent of your daily quota!

Sounds glib, but when I'm producing first drafts, especially of
academic work, I'm most often not "writing," I'm *typing*. What's
the difference between writing and typing? Typing happens
when I'm putting something down on the page, getting shit
done; writing is what happens when I'm reworking what I've

typed into stronger sentences, more shapely paragraphs, more coherent arguments. Understanding the differences between these two modes has helped me slog along through chapters and books even when what I'm typing represents a quite early stage in the development of a line of thought or piece of scholarship.

* * *

Another word for writing, then, is revision. I would guess that I spend four or five times the effort and energy revising my academic prose as I do in initially drafting it. One of the consistent practices I adopt in revision has been the careful scrutiny of my subjects and verbs during the production of final drafts. Every sentence in both my fiction and my academic writing gets parsed with a few basic questions in mind. What is the grammatical subject of this sentence—and, just as importantly, why? Should *this* subject be performing *that* action? Are there other agents and actions that might more effectively get across the substantive point I'm trying to make? What's a stronger or subtler verb I could use here? Six times out of ten the sentence will be just fine as is, the way I first typed it. But I make serious edits on nearly half of my sentences, consciously following basic and rather old-fashioned rules for good writing, such as avoiding over-reliance on to-be verbs. Whenever I use a to-be verb I do so consciously, as when I want to emphasize the two sides of a predicate nominative or predicate adjective. In those cases an *is* is exactly what I want. I can now sniff out those moments in my writing when I'm trying too hard to avoid to-be verbs. The syntax and diction tend to get crabbed, overly dense, with a strained verb or a mixed metaphor resulting from a mismatch between subject and predicate.

Yeah, mixed metaphors. Oof! They're the hallmark of tendentious, portentous academic writing. Witness an actual passage from one of my books, published about ten years ago:

> For the most part, the epistemological segregations that
> defined modernity and its regimes of knowledge production
> over the course of the twentieth century were resolutely op-
> posed to the kinds of historical self-scrutiny demanded by
> the acceptance or even the entertainment of Bruno Latour's
> corrosive proposition.

An atrocious sentence by any measure. Bloated, overly complex, reliant on an excess of subordinating constructions and
baffling overstatement. Oh, and talk about mixed metaphors!
*Segregation, regimes, self-scrutiny, acceptance, entertainment,
corrosion.* I mean, what was I even trying to say here? The
sentence substitutes verbiage for thought, tortuous syntax for
analysis. Rereading it helps me understand why I've turned
with such enthusiasm and industry to the practices of revision
described above. They've changed my academic writing style
quite radically, I hope for the better—and I wince when I
look back at the kind of prose I sometimes produced earlier
in my career. My rule now: if I can't happily read a sentence
aloud the day after I typed it, and understand in the moment
the relation of parts to whole, it gets the knife.

(Yes, I realize there have been rather fierce debates around
this issue in recent years. Polemics against the logic of "common sense," contests to identify the worst academic writing,
curmudgeonly attacks on theory masked as prim defenses
of plain speaking, and so on. Scholars I admire greatly have
made strong arguments against just the sort of critical style I
now find myself favoring and practicing. For the purposes of
this collection, though, I wanted to be honest about the issue
rather than pretending such differences of taste, style, inflec-
tion, practice, and commitment don't exist and don't affect the
choices we make as writers. So please note that I'm talking
here about how *I* write, not how others *should* write.)

How We Write catches me at a transitional moment in my writing life. I am coming to appreciate ever more deeply the power of story in shaping every piece of writing I produce, including the central critical arguments about literature and language informing my academic prose. I've become more attuned to the role of plot, suspense, and character in the unfolding of articles and book chapters (not just my own), and I've made a deliberate effort to bring out these narrative elements regardless of the subject I'm treating. I might be writing about William Caxton and his liturgical printing, or about images of uterine vellum in lyric poetry. But even in these cases I love figuring out who my protagonist should be and telling its, her, or his story in the most effective way I can—subplots, villains, and all. My protagonist in any given piece of writing might be a poem, a stanza, an author, an interpretive crux, a manuscript. At the moment she's a brown cow, an animal beloved of an early Irish saint who comes back from the dead to inscribe on this creature's skin an epic story of a cattle raid. Her hide has become a piece of parchment, you see. That's *not* how I write, thankfully, though at the moment this ageing dog is nuzzling my feet, and while I really like my laptop I'm looking at her down there, and wondering what her next life will hold.

Stuart Elden
Writing by Accumulation

Writing Regularly

Generally the advice I give on writing has been along the lines of saying "there is no one correct way to write, but there are plenty of ways people seem to be stuck in that are not working well for them." This can then lead into a discussion of different people's writing strategies, with their peculiarities, conventions, strengths and weaknesses, which may suggest things that others might find helpful, or at least worth giving a try. Such events—workshops on publishing or writing, for example—can be really helpful, and to put something similar down in book form seems a really good idea. I certainly don't want to suggest that I always get it right with my own writing, and (although people seem to have a different impression) I find writing hard. My solution to this, such as it is, is to build writing up slowly, in small manageable pieces, a little-by-little approach that can develop over time into something. And I suppose, when pressed, this is the advice I *do* give people, especially my students: do not defer writing to some point in the future, and write regularly. I admire people who seem to be able to turn on the "writing switch," and produce large quantities of material in intense bursts of creativity. But that rarely works for me, and so I've worked out a different approach. It's not like pushing pebbles off a cliff, but slowly rolling them up one, to form a small but growing pile; where frequently pebbles will be removed, polished, and rearranged, and sometimes replaced or discarded. Over time the pebbles become something, or the pile gets raided for a different pile.

IMAGE: The author's workspace. 95

Writing regularly does not mean everyday, although for me that would be the ideal situation. Writing regularly is about planning your time so that writing is there as an important aspect. I am sure that for many, writing is the activity that most regularly gets squeezed out in busy and hectic schedules. Perhaps only background or speculative reading is more commonly dropped to make time for other things. But given the importance of writing for academic careers, it is unfortunate that it gets dropped, deferred, neglected. When at my busiest—as director of graduate studies in the first year of editing *Society and Space*—I still tried to keep writing part of my regular schedule. It was the first time someone else had the ability to put meetings into my diary without my direct approval. In order to keep writing going, I would put a few times—perhaps two hours long—as appointments with myself into the diary. I would tell the people who had access to my diary that they could move them, but they could not delete them. So they could be at different times of the day or week to accommodate other things, but they were supposed not to disappear. It was difficult to maintain this, but the idea of building time into your schedule for research-based activity seemed the only way to avoid it being dropped entirely.

I firmly believe the way to write is to make time to write, and to protect it. Ideally, yes, I have completely uninterrupted time to write, and I like to block out complete days, but those can be a scarce commodity. The days are very hard to come by when teaching, and even when on research leave or fellowship other tasks such as reading PhD students' work, other projects, editing a journal, referee tasks, meetings, correspondence, etc. can intrude. My perfect writing day would be to split the day into two parts—a long uninterrupted session in the morning, followed by a long bike ride to clear the head and let ideas come, followed by another session later in the day. But such days can rarely be achieved. So, for me, the way to ensure that the writing does not continually get deferred until that "clear day" is to make time for it.

Collapsing the Research/Writing Distinction

Writing for me is not something separate from, and subsequent to, research. I don't do "research" and then write "it" up. Rather it's a continually intertwined process. I type up my notes, even if I've first taken them on paper. Having quotations and thoughts from reading in Word files, or now, increasingly, in Evernote, means that I can access the material easily. Keeping all my active research files and writing projects in Dropbox has really helped now that I am visiting other universities increasingly often because of my role at Warwick. I'm never in a work setting without at least one device I can access these files on.

So I write about my reading, commentary on and around quotations, and in this way often texts begin to emerge. In all my different projects I work mainly with texts (primary texts, secondary literature, interviews, documents, news reports etc.), so the note taking is an integral part of the writing. This helps generate things I might use. I write to make sense of what I'm writing, what I'm thinking, what I'm reading. I rarely begin writing at the beginning of a section or chapter, but often write out from some middle point. Sections begin to develop, and things get reordered. Texts emerge—I rarely sit down and begin writing "a paper" from scratch. I write, trying to remember that the sentence I am writing will not be the one that will appear on the printed published page. Nothing I write is final, which for me helps to break the block that can come with trying to get a word, phrase, sentence or paragraph "right". I try to get the gist of what I am thinking, saying, arguing down, and go back over it again and again. I edit, rewrite, edit and repeat the process. Sentences and paragraphs get broken in half, things get reordered, cut out, or written again. If I get stuck, I tend to write what I call my "stage directions" into the text, usually enclosed in square brackets and sometimes highlighted: "this bit doesn't work"; "revise this"; "add references to X"; "what's the point here?"; "does this make sense?" and so on. Then I move to the next part, knowing I will return. Things can change a lot in the process of writing, and I try to defer knowing exactly how things will turn out to as late as possible, to keep my own enthusiasm for the work.

I tend to think in terms of book length projects. For many years now I have been clearer about the next books I am planning to write than about the next article I will submit. I tend to see books as my priority, articles as interim statements of book-projects or chances to do something a little different (sometimes in collaboration). Book chapters I tend to do if they are interesting projects I'd like to be involved in, or they give me the chance to do something that I know would not work so well as a journal article. Different styles of writing can suit different projects. Some things — book reviews, for instance, or pieces like the present one — I tend to sit down and try to write from start to finish in one or two consolidated periods. But mainly it is the writing by accumulation or accretion, slowly building something up over time. What this means is that everything but very late drafts are a terrible mess — you can see the cogs and gears turning. I'd like to think that the versions I circulate for comments, and certainly those that I submit somewhere have this all cleaned up and polished. But this is one of the reasons why collaborative writing is a strange thing to do — you have to be prepared to show work in progress, with all those infelicities on display.

The Mechanics

I resave each file again each day, and sometimes even more frequently, with the date and sometimes "morning/afternoon/ evening" in the file name — "Chapter One 21 June 2015," for example — and build up an archive of old versions of material. Memory storage is cheap today, so disk space isn't an issue. If

I make radical changes to a text, and then decide someway down the line that a previous version worked better, then I can still find the relevant passage. "Undo" can be useful of course, but you can't undo selective actions instead of the whole after that point, and undo doesn't work once you have closed and reopened a file. Anything cut goes into a special file of "discards," which can be returned to at later stages—some things that needed to be cut can still prove useful at a later point. I sometimes turn "track changes" on, and then make it invisible on the screen. That way I can survey what I've done at the end of the day and return to previous formulations. I don't like seeing the changes appear, but having a chance to check back is helpful. You can do this other ways of course, but this one works for me, usually on late drafts.

If I have a time set aside for writing and the creative spark just isn't there, then I try to use the time for something connected to the work. Finding library shelfmarks, ordering books from the library store or on inter-library loan, downloading relevant articles, checking author-guidelines, and so on. Or I print the last draft and read it over for grammar, maybe seeing a link or sparking an idea. I tend to do the notes as I go, but tidying up references can also be done in less creative time. Anything that moves the writing forward is, I think, a productive use of the time. Incremental movement is still movement towards a goal. I try not to fall into the habit of just using that time for reading though, because sometimes reading, while essential, can be a deferral strategy: "if I can just get through this pile of reading, this book, those articles, then I will be ready to write." But the reading is, thankfully, something that will never be finished. Given that I don't really make a distinction between "writing" and "research," this can sometimes be blurred, but I try not to delay writing too long. Even initial sketchy thoughts on the basis of reading, followed by more reading, and more writing, can move things forward.

I've also run a blog for the last five and a bit years—
www.progressivegeographies.com. The blog has gained a respect-
able readership, in large part because I link to lots of things that I
find interesting, and so I'm aware people are reading it as a kind
of research hub. Few people can possibly be interested in all the
things I'm interested in, but more people seem to have an interest in some of them than would be following the blog if it was
just about my research. But when I do say something about my
research, there is a large audience out there who become exposed
to it. Unlike other people, I've tended not to post sections of
draft material to the blog, in the hope of comments. I admire
people who do, especially for their ability to share very tentative
initial thoughts. But for me what I've found useful is to blog
about my work, rather than blog my work. This began when I was
working on my book *The Birth of Territory*, where I would share
things I was discovering, or stories of problems with tracking
down ever more arcane references, or talk about the process
of building an argument, structuring chapters and revising the
manuscript. I found this process helpful, partly because it gave
me an opportunity to discuss the work I was doing, and to reassure myself that I had been doing something productive, even
if several days' work only appeared as a trace in the manuscript,
perhaps in an endnote. I've been doing something similar with
the writing of my current books on Foucault, with semi-regular
updates on what I've been doing.

In my writing, I quite often build up "tools" to help with
the process. So, with the *Foucault's Last Decade* book one of the
first tasks was using Daniel Defert's "Chronology" from *Dits
et écrits* as the basis for a timeline in that period. I then worked
through the lecture courses, *Dits et écrits* itself, the biographies
and other textual information to add lots of details. This pre-
paratory work was then helpful for me in seeing the proximity
of things that might otherwise appear disconnected. This then
became a constant reference as I was working on the material,

often being amended or supplemented by new information. In doing this I was able to identify some discrepancies in published material, or make connections that would have been otherwise unnoticed by me. With some other things, I made line-by-line comparisons between variant forms of a text, which served a quite specific purpose for me, but which perhaps would only figure in the finished manuscript as a minute trace. Often I shared those on my blog—I benefitted from some others doing similar work in the past, so thought it might be helpful to others to make mine available. The development of these kinds of tools—mini-concordances, bibliographies, variant texts, etc.—might be seen as separate from writing, but for me this kind of mechanical work is again part of the overall process because it is moving the writing forward.

Usually I write best in the morning, so I try to limit the distraction of email at that time, and avoid having the schedule for my day set by others. Email, editing, admin, teaching preparation etc. are things that can come later. I find I can tolerate the less appealing aspects of my work much better if I've had a daily fix of writing, or moving writing projects forward. So, if I can—in the summer, say, or when on research leave—I try to set at least a couple of hours aside with no distractions. To help with writing, I try to organize other aspects of my work life the best I can. Good email management, note software, a good RSS feed reader and so on all make a difference. Because I no longer trust myself to be undistracted, I have taken email off my main computer in my home study. I have that on my laptop, phone and iPad, but when I switch to one of them it's clear I'm no longer writing. I've also blocked Facebook and Twitter from that computer, and when working on just a laptop, use the "WasteNoTime" plug-in to block those sites and others for a set period of time or limit the time I can spend on them per day. I can always switch to the phone or the tablet, but again it's clear I'm no longer writing.

Presenting Writing

As much as possible I use conference papers or invited lectures as opportunities to move the writing tasks forward. This means that I quite often decline things that will pull me in a different direction, or give "yes, but…" replies. For several years I would accept invitations primarily if they allowed me to speak about some aspect of the history of territory project. Now I'm much more likely to take the time to prepare a talk, travel and spend time at a place if it allows me to talk about Foucault or Shakespeare, because that is where my current projects and interests are.

There are times when a conference paper or an invited seminar is just that event. But as much as I am able I try to use it as a chance to try out ideas with an audience, and to have the non-negotiable deadline of a talk as goal to aim for with the writing. What this means is that I generally *write* a talk, even if I later turn it into a presentation. I don't like reading every word of a talk, but there is generally a largely written version behind the scenes. When I have a written text, then I might turn it into a PowerPoint presentation. So the presentation comes from the text, rather than the other way round. I'm well aware lots of people do the reverse, and that it works for them. But I equally think there are lots of people with conference papers that never got elaborated, or PowerPoints that don't make sense when they revisit them months later. Planning it directly as a presentation often means it ends up as nothing more than that. PowerPoints, for me, began with a text, which I turn into a presentation—first the quotes, then some relevant images, and then the "structure" slides. I then take the written text and edit it to work as notes for the presentation, which I practice aloud a few times, breaking up the longer sentences and paragraphs; putting in marginal notes for which passages to "skip," "summarize," or "explain" more fully; and put in the cues for the slides. For me the advantage of this is that I have a fairly good text immediately after the presentation.

I then go over the notes for the presentation and incorporate the relevant ones into the master file of the text; add in notes in relation to especially good questions; etc. before I next present it to an audience. If that's very shortly afterwards then I might make the annotations for the second presentation in a different ink on the same script. But all of this exists on paper, or on file, and it's there even if I don't have time to work it into a proper text immediately. Recently I've been scanning the paper versions, with all the annotations and notes from audience questions, to a pdf and saving with the Word files.

Conclusion

For me the goal is not counting words. But think of it this way. Take a 52-week year. Take four weeks holiday. Take three days per week with time set aside for writing. That's 144 writing days. Write 500 words a day—about a page of a printed text. That's 72,000 words, which could be seen as roughly two articles and half a book. A couple of articles a year and a book every two or three isn't exactly Sartre-level words per day madness—it's an achievable amount of work. With a relatively small number of writing days a week it quickly adds up to a substantial amount. The 500 words target is good, finished, polished, and properly footnoted text. For me the way to do this is to try to write regularly, to protect writing time, to have the tools and mechanics right and to free myself from the pressure of thinking any sentence I write is the final version. As I said, I generally write, edit, rewrite, etc. multiple times, so that different parts of the writing will be at different stages.

I've written about "writing" quite a few times on the Progressive Geographies blog (and raided some of those posts for a few sentences here), in part because I'm very interested in how different people do this. I'm not trying to convince anyone my way should be their way, but maybe something in how I work might spark an idea that is different. Derek Gregory, for example, works in a quite different way from me, often beginning with the idea of a presentation, a storyboard, and images, and crafting a narration to go with this, which over time becomes a written text. It clearly works for him—an excellent presenter and prolific writer. Henry Yeung and I did a session on writing strategies when I was visiting National University of Singapore, and we work in very different ways, only agreeing that we'd found a system that works for us. Graham Harman and I have discussed our very different approaches on our respective blogs. Collaborative writing—with Neil Brenner, Jeremy Crampton, Luiza Bialasiewicz, Eduardo Mendieta, Adam David Morton and others has taught me how different people work, and how to integrate different approaches. What matters is to find a way that works for you; and to be willing to experiment once in a while. I suspect most people who are now broadly happy with how they work would suggest that it is something they have arrived at over time, rather than how they have always worked. I've written this piece in a very different way to my normal practice, and found some aspects of that refreshing. I am sure I will learn other approaches from the other contributions to this book.

off at midnight. Every day for...

work like that again. Years later, while I was writing *The Colonial Present*, I became
wholly absorbed in the attempt to keep up with a cascade of real-time events in multiple
places. My training as an historical geographer hadn't prepared me for that – I'd always
envied the ability of colleagues writing about contemporary issues to make sense of a
world that was changing around them as they wrote – and there were times when I
yearned for the less frenetic pace of archival work. But I wasn't writing to a deadline
(though as the project swelled beyond an analysis of the US-led invasion of Afghanistan
to include Israel's renewed assault on occupied Palestine and then the US-led invasion
of Iraq, I decided I must finish before Bush invaded France).

Deadlines are the problem: I've always had the greatest difficulty writing to meet them
because I can never be sure where my words will take me. Lecturing is something else

---

Travelling through words

Derek Gregory

The way I write – by which I mean both the practices I follow and (please God) the style
of my writing – has changed over the years; though, as I tell all my students, that doesn't
mean it's become any easier.

I wrote my PhD thesis in three weeks. There. I said it. And it's true. Three we[eks]
starting at 7 a.m., with 30 minutes off for lunch (including a walk to the corner sh[op]
a newspaper, trailed by our deeply suspicious cat all the way there and all the way [back]
an hour off for dinner and the quick pleasure of a novel, knocking off a [mid]nigh[t]
day for 21 days. When I finished I vowed never to work like that again. I've a[lways had]
the greatest difficulty writing to deadlines because I can never be sure wher[e my words]
will take me, but lecturing is something else entirely. There's something in...
pressing about facing a live audience the next morning, and since I don't...
prepared script I don't have to fine-tool my prose or curb my flights of...
the sense of freedom that gives me. In those pre-digital days you co[uld]...
raft of excuses to keep you afloat in the face of turbulent editors – ...
the flotsam of 'I posted it last week'. But a PhD thesis combine[s]...
worlds: appealing to a mail-storm was out of the question...
examiners were live and all too close at hand. The problem wa[s]
real progress on my research and had instead devoted myself...
again). Every Wednesday evening I would walk home after re...
start next morning. But who starts on a Thursday?
...[d]ay evening found me walking ho[me]
...and who sta[rted]

ght buil[t]
is PhD
cked up in a
it done to
owa. In the
10 days.
ost
ver known,

Derek Gregory
Travelling Through Words

The way I write—by which I mean both the practices I follow
and (please God) the style of my writing—has changed over
the years: though, as I tell all my students, that doesn't mean it's
become any easier.

I wrote my PhD thesis (on the woolen industry in Yorkshire
between 1780 and 1840) in three weeks. Really. Starting at 7 A.M.,
with thirty minutes off for lunch (including a walk to the corner
shop for a newspaper, trailed by our deeply suspicious cat all the
way there and all the way back), an hour off for dinner and the
quick pleasure of a novel, knocking off at midnight. Every day
for twenty-one days. When I finished I promised myself I'd never
work like that again. Years later, while I was writing *The Colonial
Present*, I became wholly absorbed in the attempt to keep up
with a cascade of real-time events in multiple places. My training
as an historical geographer hadn't prepared me for that—I'd
always envied the ability of colleagues writing about contemporary issues to make sense of a world that was changing around
them as they wrote—and there were times when I yearned for
the less frenetic pace of archival work. But I wasn't writing to a
deadline—though as the project swelled beyond an analysis of
the US-led invasion of Afghanistan to include Israel's renewed
assault on occupied Palestine and then the US-led invasion of
Iraq, I decided I must finish before Bush invaded France.

Deadlines are the problem: I've always had the greatest difficulty writing to meet them because I can never be sure where my

I am immensely grateful to Trevor Barnes and Craig Jones
for commenting on a draft of this essay.

IMAGE: Edits to this text.   107

words will take me. Lecturing is something else entirely. There's something infinitely more pressing about facing a live audience the next morning, and since I don't perform from a prepared script I don't have to fine-tool my prose or curb my flights of fancy, and I like the sense of freedom that gives me. Anyone writing in those pre-digital days could also rely on a raft of excuses to stay afloat in the face of turbulent editors—not least clinging to the flotsam of "I posted the manuscript last week." But a PhD thesis combined the worst of both worlds: appealing to a mail-storm was out of the question, and my Cambridge examiners were live and all too close at hand. The problem was that I had made little real progress and instead had devoted myself to acting (a live audience again). Every Wednesday evening I would walk home after rehearsals promising myself a fresh start the following morning. But who starts on a Thursday? So we agreed, me and I, to wait until Monday. Monday evening found me walking home after rehearsals renewing my vows. But it was the 29th of the month, and who starts anything then? So we both agreed to wait until the 1st of the month. And when that arrived, it was a Thursday. You could keep this up forever, or at least I could. In this case, the back story was that I had been married for just three months when my mother-in-law offered to take my wife for an extended visit to her family in Colombia, and I realized that this was an opportunity for uninterrupted, distraction-free writing.

Those two adjectives tell the real story: how I welcomed those interruptions and distractions! There always seemed to be good reasons to defer putting pen to paper (or, more accurately in those days, fingers to the keys of my electric typewriter). As you will have gathered I was, and remain, a past master at procrastination. I know that many writers have an iron will and obediently follow a strict self-discipline. Perhaps the most extreme, though sadly apocryphal, example is Victor Hugo, who supposedly instructed his manservant to confiscate all his clothes so that he couldn't leave the house while he was working on a novel. But that's not me (I don't have a manservant).

Or at any rate, it's not me until I immerse myself in the writing. And that's always been my first problem: starting. Over the years I've learned to know and trust myself. So I know I can write in the morning, sometimes in the evening but never in the afternoon—so I've stopped trying. And if the words aren't there on Monday morning, there is no point in spending the day staring at the screen and hesitantly pecking at the keys, because I know very well that the next morning I will come in, read the print-out and tear the whole thing up. Better to find other things to do—especially if I can convince myself that they are getting me into the right space to start the next day. The converse is also true. If the words are leaking out of my fingertips dismally early on a Sunday morning, then out they must come (and, in case you are wondering, I'm still married to my wife—who learned all this long before I did). The irony is that once the text is moving, I've always wondered why it took me so long to get started.

I invariably wonder about that because I actually enjoy the process once it's under way, though each time I also wonder whether I'll be able to pull it off again. Whenever I sit at my desk, or increasingly these days my laptop, there's almost always a flicker of doubt: will the words come this time? I imagine (another conceit, I know) that it's something like the moment just before the diver launches himself into space. I pause, waiting to break the still surface of the screen.

I have my own swimming-pool library, of course. I'll have read and read and then read some more, and I'll have organized my notes, quotations, comments, thoughts and ideas into a long working—I was going to say draft, but it's more of a storyboard. In the past, the storyboard would have been the product of reading and thinking, by which I mean it was a verbal-textual product-in-formation. Reading is a creative process, to be sure, though it's usually an internal one as you work with the text to understand what the author is arguing (and why they could possibly be arguing *that*) while at the same time making it your own: not just putting it into your own words but working out what you make of it, where it's taking you (and whether you want to go there), and installing it into your own library (where it may well magically move from one shelf to another). So I've got endless notes — Kindle Highlights now saves me hours of transcription, and I work through them, highlighting key passages in bold, adding comments and organizing them into digital files — and I'll have extracted what I need, and cut-and-pasted everything into a rough map that still doesn't commit me to any single route.

I know that it's also a long way from the text I'm going to write; I open that up as a separate document, control my fear at its blankness by formatting the page, giving the document a title (I actually can't write without a title), saving it, and then — well, wait or write.

I don't read (or write) with a single purpose; on the way all sorts of other ideas flicker into being, rarely fully formed, that might end up in the essay I'm working on at the moment but might just as well end up as the spur for something else altogether. My sources are all over the place, and ideas are as likely to emerge from fiction as they are from anywhere else. Years ago I read William Boyd's *An Ice-Cream War*, and one passage — "Gabriel thought maps should be banned. They gave the world an order and reasonableness it didn't possess" — stayed with me, like a burr clinging to my jeans. I used it as an epigraph in one of the chapters in *Geographical Imaginations*, but years later I surprised myself by returning not only to that passage but also to the incident it described, and unfolding it into a completely new essay on cartographic vision and what I called "corpography" in the First World War (in which another novel, Tom McCarthy's *C*, also occupies a central place: I can't think of a more beautiful combination of skilled research and superb writing). I called the essay "Gabriel's Map" — of course — but, more figuratively for my present purposes, working on it confirmed that there's something deeply deceptive about mapping, a false sense of security that has to be supplemented by lively interruptions activated through the body.

So I also like to be free of the text—springing away from the board, if you like (and I do like)—so that for me there's always been another moment in creative work that is an intensely physical, even corporeal process, thinking that is best conducted on the move, sometimes in front of a class but often out walking, alive to the world around me until it disappears into my own fabricated world. I've always had the sensation of *feeling* myself think: of ideas moving around, words forming in my mouth, whole phrases springing to my lips (the real trick is to remember them!). I often talk to myself, even say passages out loud, because the rhythm and cadence of the prose matters to me, and I know it does to some readers too. I remember Roger Lee, when he was editor of the *Transactions of the Institute of British Geographers*, writing to tell me that he had just spent a summer's afternoon wandering around his garden reading aloud parts of my manuscript on the Egyptian journeys of Florence Nightingale and Gustave Flaubert. It was a characteristically thoughtful and wonderfully appreciative remark, and I've never forgotten it. In some measure, I think, I always have Roger and his garden in my mind's eye as I try to coax more words into the world.

Even writing is a corporeal process. I can't think with my laptop on my lap—it has to be on a table or a desk—and I need a chair that I can push back or pull up; I need space to get up, scoot to a book-case, stand and gaze out of the window; and I write best in bare feet (seriously: perhaps that's where the diving metaphor comes from). I usually write three or four pages without much editing. This is never the whole argument or story, just the first three or four pages, and—like those crime novelists whose work I most admire—I'm never sure where I'm going next. (How I despair of those who tell me they have finished their research so that all—all!—they have to do is "write it up," as though writing is not part of the creative research process: if what you've written is merely a record of what you've done or thought, then perhaps you should work in a laboratory). Three or four hot pages uncurl from the printer, and then I take myself off—sometimes to my office at the university, sometimes to a coffee shop—where I go over what I've written. It's much better editing hard copy than trying to do so on the screen, and for some reason I have to use a black roller-ball; pencil doesn't work, and blue ink is a disaster. By the time I've re-written the draft, expanded sentences that I now see are shorthand for something that needs much more explication, and added notes to myself about work that needs to be done to fill out gaps, I've also got a sense of where the writing is taking me next.

So it's back to the keyboard—and back to the beginning of the manuscript. I rework my original pages, and by the time I've finished (scribbling on my original storyboard and annotating the map while I'm writing the essay, adding footnotes which will sometimes make it into the finished version but are just as likely to be notes to myself, and pushing further out into the unknown) those three or four pages will have grown to six or seven. I use footnotes constantly, sometimes as commentary, often as placeholders for paragraphs to be drafted in the next round of revisions, and always as a holding pen for references. I never use the Harvard reference system while I'm composing—to me, the arch-enemy of good writing—and the final labor of transforming (deforming) my prose into the obstacle course of brackets, names and dates required by most journals is the most depressing part of the whole business.[1] Once my six or seven pages are on the screen the cycle starts again: back to the beginning, editing, annotating, moving some of those footnotes

1   Derek Gregory, "Editorial," in *Environment and Planning D: Society and Space* 8 (1990), 1-6.

into the text (which is often the best place for them) and composing another three or four pages, slowly pushing on.

It's a discontinuous process, but I'm always writing from the beginning towards the end, although I never know in advance where that will be. It isn't seamless, and sometimes everything comes to a juddering halt. These days I use my blog as (among other things) a sort of five-finger exercise, practicing ideas for long-form essays and getting the words to flow across the screen, but some days that's not enough. In fact, I can look back at virtually all of my published work and remember how the gaping white space between this paragraph and that marks a week, sometimes (far) longer, when nothing was working. That's almost always been because I didn't know enough or because I'd tried to dodge a difficulty. So I eventually admit to myself that I need to read and think some more, to go back and undo the preceding paragraphs, even—the horror of it!—to delete whole passages (that's easily the hardest part, but I've learned to save those deletions in case they can be given a new lease of life somewhere else), and often to re-order or even re-think the narrative. This also usually involves going off to find new source materials, reading more essays and more books, so that the whole journey opens up again. En route, my desk becomes steadily more cluttered with piles of books, previous print-outs, pages from articles and far too many black roller-ball pens. There's no trail of breadcrumbs to take me back to the beginning, but there are several coffee mugs in different stages of decomposition which mark the stages of my increasing immersion in the text. Friends and family know when I'm not working on something: my desk is tidy. But once I'm in that space (the zone?) I never, ever stop the research and switch to writing.

I've described all this as working with a storyboard, largely because I think of what I do now as telling stories. This means two things. First, I think it's a mistake to front-load theory into any essay; unless what you are about is textual exegesis—I did a lot of that in the past, but if I do it now it's *en passant*—that act will needlessly limit the story you tell. You may think that's a good thing—after all, you can't say everything and you need to keep what you write within bounds—but I've come to think of writing as a journey that takes me (and, crucially, my readers) to unexpected places. Front-loading theory is the intellectual equivalent of a conjurer coming on stage and showing the audience how a trick is done before they do it. There's a reason they don't do that. I realize that this *is* a device which helps a lot of writers magic words onto the page, but it gives the impression that theory is something to be "applied," that it provides a template, whereas I try to treat it as a *medium* in which I work—and one that will be changed by the substantive materials I use. (In much the same way, my "map" is constantly changed as I travel with it: it's not the map but the *mapping* that matters). I also think that the best sort of theory is carried in solution: if you know your Michel Foucault or Judith Butler, say, you will recognize their hand in what I write, but if you don't you are not disqualified from grasping what I'm saying. It follows, too, that theory in my writing is always impure and hybrid; I borrow from multiple sources, since I still haven't found anyone who asks all the interesting questions or provides all the satisfying answers, and I'm usually aware of the tensions and contradictions between them. But ultimately the story is the thing.

Second, writing is no longer a purely verbal-textual process for me because I now work from a visual storyboard. Everything I've written for the past five or six years (apart from this essay, ironically) has emerged out of presentations that I've tried to design to make as visually arresting as possible. I've found a real pleasure in image research—which often takes me to sources I would never have found any other way, and opens up avenues of inquiry I'd never have glimpsed otherwise—but it's also a way of "slow thinking": of trying to work out how best to show what I mean, and even of figuring out *what* I mean. One of Allan Pred's favourite Benjamin quotations was "I have nothing to say, only to show,"[2] and at long last I'm discovering the power of that resonant phrase. So as I search for images, and juggle text boxes and fonts, I'm thinking about how this will *look* and *in consequence* what it will say…instead of lines of text marching across the screen, words appearing from I never know quite where, everything slows down and, again, I *feel myself think*. I've found this even more immersive than pure writing, a process of creation that constantly draws me in and draws me back and pushes me on. It's also interactive: it's much easier to re-jig a presentation, which I do every time depending on the previous audience's reaction and the Q&A, than it is to re-work a text (and reading a paper to an audience is in most cases one of the least effective ways of communicating anything of substance to anyone). I should probably add that I prefer Keynote to PowerPoint, I never use preset templates and there's not a bullet point in sight. Since I don't have a script to accompany the presentation, the only disadvantage is that once I've performed the thing enough times for me to be more or less satisfied with the argument, at least for the moment, I then have to convert a cascade of images and quotations into a text.…Sometimes, to be honest, that means I don't; I've done the fun part, and I shrink from the labor of conversion. Sometimes I do—in which case the whole process starts all over again, using the presentation as the basis for the storyboard and adding more notes, ideas and sources to track down.

There's also another, more traditional sense of interactivity involved in my work, because there comes a time when writing has to join up with reading: communication is, after all, a collaborative not a competitive process. So I've always relied on good friends (colleagues and graduate students alike) who are willing to read my far too long drafts and tell me exactly what they

2   Allan Pred, *Recognizing European Modernities: A Montage of the Present* (London: Routledge, 1995), 11.

disagree with, what they don't get, and what is wrong with them; they almost always suggest other things to think about and other sources to track down. Referees are often a different kettle of fish, particularly if you haven't referred to them (which is what some of them seem to think "refereeing" means). But here too there is an opportunity for dialogue—there's no point in acceding to every criticism and suggestion if you're not persuaded by them, and I've learned most from those editors who have identified the points which they think are particularly sharp while leaving me to make up my own mind so long as I can justify it.

In this sense, writing—like reading—can be a never-ending process. In much the same way that you can't read the same book twice, because you are no longer the same person that read it first time round, you read your own work differently when you see it through someone else's eyes. And that's one of the best things about the whole process. There are times when writing *is* a solitary and remarkably lonely affair. There's a passage at the very end of E.P. Thompson's *Whigs and Hunters*—one of my political and intellectual heroes ever since I worked on my PhD—where he describes himself sitting in his study, the clock ticking towards midnight, the desk covered with notes and drafts. I identify with that; but there is also that wonderful moment when you are released back into the world that lies outside the text—with your text in your hands *and* in your reader's. There's no greater reward.

Steve Mentz
Wet Work: Writing as Encounter

I never know what will happen when I sit down to write.

* * *

Writing's the hardest and most urgent thing we do as academics. I don't think my combination of sportstalk, swimming, and Renaissance intellectual history translates into anything like advice. But I love this book's idea of sprawling our weirdnesses out on pages and screens for everyone to see.

* * *

For this child of the New Jersey suburbs, sports still has the best metaphors. Here's one I start with:

Writing Maxim #1: "Swing hard, in case you hit the ball."

The baseball metaphor highlights chance and difficulty: some key parts of the writing process, as I semi-understand it, remain out of the author's control. The maxim encourages getting comfortable with failure, because that's what happens most of the time. So much of writing feels like chance and failure—you practice and practice, get your swing just right, hope for contact, and most of the time you miss the ball. Writing isn't about control, no matter how hard we work at it. "You can't aim the baseball," intones the sonorous announcer's voice that accompanies me on my evening commute from April to (if we're lucky) October. It takes all your skill just to make contact, and then hope something good happens. If not, take another swing.

IMAGE: Photo of the author swimming courtesy of Olivia Mentz.

119

Giving up control keeps my fingers moving, loosely attached to or sometimes ahead of my thoughts. All I need to do is wiggle my fingers, initiate the encounter, move the words foreword. "Shitty first drafts," says the always-wise Annie Lamott. It's an invitation to start laying words out in rows. Momentum feels like the most powerful force a writer can cultivate. I think of cultivating momentum rather than building habits or (more egotistically) practicing self-discipline, because momentum emphasizes impersonality. It's not me, not only me, doing this work. "We should say 'it's thinking,' as we say, 'it's raining,'" speculates Borges, who's always right. He's talking about writing as a form of discovery, an encounter with something we don't know yet, making something new, which is the best writing there is.

* * *

Writing Maxim #2: "What is good belongs to no one… but rather to language" (Borges).

There's something impersonal and alien about words on a page, even if it's just a computer screen. Just look at these words I've already written now, almost five hundred of them, as I sit on Delta flight 400 eastbound from Portland to JFK, trying not to jostle elbows with the young couple next to me on the first leg of their first trip to Paris. Words assume monumental form on this glowing screen. Am I responsible for all of them? Or are they just patterns predictably extracted from the storehouse of the English language?

Letting words be impersonal means that once they're on pages they're gone, neither mine nor yours nor anyone's, not entirely. That's a humbling thought, but it makes me feel free, and able to keep swinging.

* * *

As a grad student in the 1990s, I found academic publishing alien and terrifying. Some of that flavor remains. The various stages—querying a journal or press, sending out a manuscript, peer review, copy editing, page proofs—sounded then like an arcane language I was convinced everyone but me had spoken since childhood. (I suspect I was responding to the fairly high number of second-generation academics in my cohort; they knew much more than I did.) My graduate program operated through a code of silence more than explicit instructions—not an empathetic or terribly ethical pedagogy, though a powerful one—and I hesitated before sending my work to journals.

I had a stop and start experience with those early articles. On the hesitate-then-rush principle, which I don't recommend, I sent out three articles quickly in a vain effort to publish before going on the job market. They met silence, and delay, followed by more silence. I'd been acculturated to silence, so I didn't pursue the matter. Then, suddenly and too late, two were accepted, two weeks after I received my first job offer, i.e., after they could no longer do me any immediate good. The third of the three was delayed so long (no journal-shaming here, I'll hide the name) that its byline is actually my second (and current) appointment rather than the first.

Now that I've sat on the other side of the editor's desk, I'm sympathetic to delays and unfortunate timing. Publishing now looks less like a mysterious cabal governed by a secret language than a bunch of harried humans scrambling to keep the pieces together. It would have helped to have had someone say that to me in the 1990s.

Knowing what I know now about publishing demystifies the process and defuses at least some writerly paranoia. But it also makes me wonder: what if paranoia, pressure, anxiety, is what makes me write? What if I need that push, the nearness of failure, the half-step of the stair that isn't there? The pressure of mostly not-hitting the ball is liberating, and also frightening.

My favorite living novelist talks about "operational paranoia," a kind of working mid-point between utter paralysis and the meaningless egoism of an anti-paranoid assimilation of world into self. I love Pynchon's extended recognition, which has taken him through several thousand of pages of baroque prose, silly names, and manic plotting, that operational paranoia is uncomfortable and inescapable. We write in and through anxieties from which we can't and don't really want to escape—we might even, poor perverse bulbs, find ourselves enjoying them.

* * *

Writing Maxim #3: Festina lente.

For these purposes I'll slightly mistranslate the first adage in Erasmus's massive sixteenth-century compilation, *Adagia*, as "First slow, then fast, then slow again." It's usually translated "make haste slowly," but I'm emphasizing a slightly different relationship between speed and slowness. Erasmus, absurdly productive polymath, helps me think about every academic writer's bugbear: procrastination. We're a hard-working subculture, but we are also prone to being distracted by procrastinating work, like, say, writing a short essay on writing in response to a conversation that developed out of a Facebook-and-blog exchange when you should be writing that overdue article on early modern hurricanes. The oxymoronic structure of *Festina lente* suggests that slowness can be rethought as preparation, a necessary precursor and contrast to speed—and vice versa. Haste makes slowness; slowness fuels haste. We need both, and especially the transition from one to the other. This mingling of stasis and movement does not resemble a linear industrial model of production, nor the neoliberal internet-fast extrapolation of that industrial model. Writing draws squiggly lines, not straight ones. That's OK. It's good not to move only in straight lines. I know many of us, including me, have to file annual reports filled with extrapolations and predictions of what we'll write next year. Plus funding applications often imagine long, straight, triumphant progresses from idea to book. It's helpful in these cases to have a background in creative writing, and to not take bureaucracies too seriously. These systems need words, but they can get by without perfect truth.

Here's the thing: you can only write what you're ready to write, in a moment, in the encounter. You can't aim the baseball. You can prepare yourself—block off time, face the page or keyboard, assemble notes and outlines, sit pinioned in a too-small airplane seat—but you can't control what happens in the writing moment. I don't know what's happening in this moment, now, not entirely. That's the good news: it's through writing that humanists create new knowledge. It's good to surprise ourselves, when we can.

Distraction promotes discovery, which is what we really want. We write by encountering our environments, by which I mean, among other things, wind and water and earth, and also the intellectual swirl of ideas and words, curated these days often enough by the Blue Faceworld of Mark Zuckerberg, whose algorithm brought me to Michael Collins's Facebook post and later to Suzanne Conklin Akbari and Alexandra Gillespie's In the Middle blog post. The intense distractions of one's own emotional climate and domestic life impinge on writing—how could they not? Speaking for myself anyway, I don't want to wall them off. I've been looking since I was a student for better ways to let the world in, to use scholarship and research and archives and detailed, technical footnotes to speak to the whole world— because what else is worth writing about, and to? The reason I'm a professor is because I'm chasing a dream in which my intellectual passions and professional requirements coincide, mostly, some of the time, at least when I hit the ball.

I've got a picture, somewhere, that must have been taken in February 2001. I'm drafting a paper for the Shakespeare Association of America conference about economic thinking in *The Merchant of Venice*. (You can find a later version of it in the 2003 collection *Money and the Age of Shakespeare*, edited by Linda Woodbridge.) In the picture, I'm sitting in a chair with a paperback open to Launcelot Gobbo's great speech about the pleasures of being an unscrupulous middle-man: "The fiend gives the more friendly counsel, I will run, fiend, my heels are at your commandment" (2.2.1–32). On my shoulder is my month-old son, red-faced and screaming. A colicky infant, he gave us about three or four hours of high-volume serenade each day for his first year or so. I was reading my paper to him—I'd started with *The Odyssey* in the hospital, sentimentalist that I am—and writing it at the same time. Surely some of his rage and force found its way into my sentences. I thought I was writing about the "new economic criticism," about which I didn't really know that much, except what I'd just started reading. But the picture shows that I was writing with and to him. In other words: rage and love, along with money and exchange.

It'd be easy to look at that picture and say I was distracted, and to think that the only responsible and professional way to write a "real" SAA paper would be in a quiet space, preferably a library carrel or a child-free office. But I don't think that would have birthed a better paper, even if I had been able to find such a place that noisy winter. The shock of fatherhood was so new to me then—he's fourteen now, but it still feels new—that there's no way I could have not been writing about it, through it, with it. I remember being frustrated that the paper wasn't as polished as I could have wished—I didn't really know at that point about the multiple drafts and revisions between conference paper and published article; another practical secret I could have benefitted from hearing earlier. But now I think of that paper as a transition, the first writing I did as a parent, an introduction to the distracted and emotional way I've been writing and living ever since.

* * *

What if we think of writing as an encounter with all the alien environments outside us? When I think about writing as process, metaphorically and physically, I return to the central obsession of my recent work, the human encounter with an alien globe best represented (to me, anyway) by the ocean. But the wet work of writing also includes encounters with an infant's scream or an indecipherable manuscript. There's no "right" way to pursue this encounter and make words from it, only a series of techniques through which we can put off being overwhelmed. Writing emerges from putting little bodies in contact with vast seas. If we try too hard to stay in control we're treating language as a mere tool, something we can master. Words are the best machines humans have constructed, but they are also perhaps our least ready to hand, most mystifying and frustrating. Wet work: it's through our efforts to employ language that we're reminded most insistently of the limits of body and mind.

Writing is like fishing in that it involves flashing a lure into the unknown and hoping that something bites. It also resembles fishing in that there's a wanton cruelty to dragging living meanings up to the surface so that we can see them. Sometimes it feels as if they should stay in the water.

Writing like swimming requires a naked encounter with unimaginable seas. I started writing about the sea by way of Northrop Frye and James Cameron: an odd combination. The great Canadian professor joked that shipwreck was the "standard means of transportation" in Greek romances and their early modern imitators (Sidney, Greene, Lodge, Nashe) about whom I wrote my dissertation and first book. The American filmmaker's sugar-sweet movie about the great ship going down showed me that shipwreck retains its potency even inside melodrama, not secret so much as unspoken, because it doesn't require words.

Writing as swimming floats in the cold water where Leo goes down. It treads water happily, patiently, knowingly, waiting for insight. It's not comfortable and it can't last. We're not in control.

Which brings me, though I hadn't started out planning to write about it, to the discomfort of writing. It's painful and exhausting. Sometimes it feels closer to drowning than swimming.

That discomfort, by the way, is one of the reasons I have begun in recent years to distract myself in sociable forms: social media, blogs, and even short essays like this one provide warmer waters in which to splash around. Like many FB-ers, I worry about the tyranny of the "like," but I also value the minor league quality of social media, where you can get a few extra swings in at words and ideas. People are watching, of course, because people are always watching. But that's OK. We're all "friends," except I guess on Twitter.

Sometimes I joke that I do my best writing without my clothes on. By that I mean that I spend a lot of time in the water thinking about sentences and words. I use daily swims to turn over sentences as I go back and forth, flipping my body over at each end of the pool. As Diana Nyad says, swimming is a form of sensory deprivation—underwater there's no smell or hearing, limited vision, only chlorine taste and enveloping anonymous touch. I use that space to compose, and try not to forget what I've been mulling when I dry off. Open water swims launch larger-scale projects.

* * *

I think formal variety is great training for academic writers. The digital media transformations we're living through seem very likely to add alternatives the traditional monograph/journal article forms that have dominated the academic landscape for some time. Today I write lots of things I wasn't trained to write in graduate school: blog posts, informal essays about writing, tweets, "swim poems." Sometimes the little things feel solvable when the big ones don't. A day when I write a 750-word blog review of a new production of Shakespeare isn't an entirely wasted day; I may not be hitting big-league pitching, but the ball is moving out of the infield. This sort of writing is lower stakes than more formal venues, but I suspect, if the truth were told, that it reaches at least as many readers, at least in the near term.

That's why I'm writing this essay when I should be working on the hurricane chapter. Small fun things keep your fingers, words, and mind working at times when you can't face the larger mountains.

* * *

I started playing with the "Swim Poem" subgenre a year or two ago, as a kind of placeholder into which to pour inchoate thoughts. It's fun to invent or encounter a new form, in which I don't feel burdened by professionalism or history or too much knowing what I'm doing. I've written about a half-dozen so far. The form lets me play outside my usual prosy modes. These lyrics build space at or across the self-world boundary, a border-crossing division that surfaces ideas. I don't always write them while I'm wet—in fact, this one is getting its first draft in the dry air of 40,000 feet. A later draft will comprise part of my BABEL 2015 project, "A Book of Absent Whales," co-created with the artist Patrick Mahon. But I think it fits here too: sounding is breathing and also writing.

Sounding

Neither in nor out, at least not always
But splashing across and through, from a circular motion
    around my shoulders
I move.
Machine-like is how I seek to feel,
Smoothly turning, as if under my outstretched fingers
    the water
Solidifies, pushes back against my palm,
Grips me as I grip it.
All too often my head turns perpendicular,
Seeking the air I share with whales
And also with this machine over which my fingers move.
What is "sounding"? Can you hear it?
Does it make pages?
Or is it simply
The noise flesh makes moving through water,
The hiss and slither of universal infamy, which will make
    itself heard
If anyone cares to listen.

Daniel T. Kline
Writing (Life): 10 Lessons

How I write is intertwined with *why I write* and ultimately constrained by *the conditions under which I write*. For me, learning, writing, and teaching have become increasingly integrated, and my academic work exists on a spectrum with the other kinds of institutionally mandated and academically required writing. Like all things, my writing process has changed as my ability to write has developed, adapting as it must to life conditions, time constraints, and workload requirements. I've never had any luck with writing schedules, but deadlines motivate me, and I've learned to adapt my writing process to the time I have available. Writing takes on the form of triage.

I think that like many of us writing for me is the place both where I examine the hidden parts of myself, reaching deep and meaningful insight, and where I encounter the deepest moments of anxiety, exposing something primal and fragile. It is the place where I am my most authentic and yet my most contrived, never quite reaching the ideal I have in my mind. Writing is a constant negotiation with grief.

1979–83: Huntsville

After flirting with physics for two years as an undergraduate at the University of Alabama in Huntsville (1979–83), I turned toward a double major in English and History after reading *Sir Gawain and the Green Knight* with William F. Munson in my sophomore-level British literature survey. It was the coolest thing I had ever read, and I'd been a reader all my life. I figured that if I were going to study literature, it might be helpful to learn about the history of the era in which the literature was rooted. UAH in those days had a strange calendar and credit system: We got semester credit for ten-week terms, and as a double humanities major, I often had four courses where—again at that time—the course requirements consisted of a midterm, a final, and a twenty-page research paper. That accelerated schedule taught me to identify a writing topic early by following a hunch, research it quickly, read about it as much as I could (in an era before online access to sources), and then get to writing because if I didn't start a couple of those papers early in the term, I'd never pass the course. I'd just jump in with a vague sense of a thesis or a series of connections that just felt right, and then I'd discover the point or work out the argument as I went. Finally, I'd revise the paper's opening to match what I'd discovered by the end, and the introduction often the last thing I'd write. It was not sophisticated, but it worked. This was before the advent of desktop computing, and while I'd taken typing in high school (during football season, when my hands were gnarled and swollen), I didn't have a typewriter of my own, so I paid $2.00 per page to have my handwritten papers typed up in the MLA or Chicago (Turabian) style. I can still feel the onion skin paper clean and slick in my hand.

> *Lesson One in How I (Continue to Learn to) Write*
> KEY: Jump in.
> PROCESS: Get a hunch, research a bit, dive in, work
>   it out, revise the introduction to fit what I've
>   already written, and move to the next paper.
>   Learn to love the bound volumes of the annual
>   *MLA Bibliography*.
> TECHNOLOGY: pen and pencil, tape, and scissors; cut
>   and paste. IBM Selectric (but not my own).
> STORAGE SYSTEM: Xerox copies & file folders.

1983–85: Huntsville

My academic journey progressed through two Master's degrees, one in English at UAH (1983–85) and the second a Master of Divinity at the Southern Baptist Theological Seminary in Louisville, Kentucky (1985–89). At UAH, I earned my MA while working as a co-op technical writer with the US Army Corps of Engineers in Huntsville. A co-op program is designed as a paid internship and meant that during one quarter, a group of four MA students worked as tech writers at the Corps, taking one course and working full-time. The following quarter, a different group of four cycled into the full-time writing position while the first group took courses full-time, still paid for by the Corps. During Reagan's Star Wars initiative, the US Army Engineer Division, Huntsville, was hopping with Cold War enthusiasm and paranoia. I worked on documents that did everything from telling facilities managers how much space and what kind of storage they needed to house weapon systems to experimental results of subnuclear testing and just about everything in between. I learned to use the *Government Printing Office Style Guide* and the coordinating regulations of the US Army, Department of Defense, and NATO. I marked up documents with a red pencil and took the revisions to the first computer lab I'd ever encountered, where the steno pool converted the marked up cut-and-paste texts into digital format and stored the documents on floppy disks, literal 8-inch "floppy" disks. Engineers and professionals of all sorts looked to us as the writing experts who could translate their technical world to others. We called ourselves "Narrative Engineers."

> *Lesson Two*
> KEY: Learn how shift gears.
> PROCESS: Writing is a set of skills that can be applied to
> any kind of text so long as you have a specific pur-

pose, a clear audience, and the proper structure
in hand. It is essentially the development of clarity.
TECHNOLOGY: Red pen, paper, and scissors; early
computer lab.
STORAGE SYSTEM: 8-inch (truly) floppy disks; Xerox
copies & file boxes.

1985–89: Huntsville & Louisville

In a place where New Criticism reigned supreme and before High
Theory ascended, we looked for patterns of imagery, and I wrote
about "images of enclosure" in Middle English literature. While
I thought I was identifying things "in the text," I was also writing about myself, my life, and my break with the fundamentalist
Christianity that had held me in thrall. But I did read Derrida's
"Structure, Sign, and Play" with David Neff, and that was chaotic
and cool. Instead of moving directly into a PhD program at that
point, I went to seminary to continue to work out those personal
issues. In a ninety-four credit hour program, the MDiv required
three interrelated tracks of study: biblical, theological, and
language study; a professional track; and free electives. I took a
degree in pastoral counseling and worked for a time with chron-
ically mentally ill young adults, working through the parallel process issues that came with having grown up with a bipolar father.
The right-wing fundamentalists took over the SBTS Board of
Regents as I finished my degree, and within three years all the
"liberal" Baptists I'd studied with were gone, tenured or not. I'd
bought my first computer in 1983, a portable Kaypro II with a
9-inch green phosphorescent screen and two 5¼-inch disk drives,
each with 360Kb of storage, and a 9-pin dot matrix printer with
that printer paper with the holes on the side. That rig cost me
$2500 and got me through two Master's degrees. I can still hear
the sizzling sound of that dot matrix printer laboriously and

eternally churning through a paper while I waited to turn it in, late for class, because the feed sprockets in the printer failed to advance the paper and printed twenty pages on a single line.

> *Lesson Three*
> KEY: Always look for the writable angle.
> PROCESS: Follow that hunch because it usually means
>   something good that is personally meaningful;
>   research and read a lot more and begin to theorize
>   and historicize the topic; but now focus the thesis, on
>   the structure flowing out of the thesis, and on revising
>   throughout the process because, you know, technology.
> TECHNOLOGY: Kaypro II (portable!).
> STORAGE SYSTEM: 5¼-inch (still floppy) disks; Xerox copies
>   & more boxes.

1990–97: Louisville & Bloomington

When I began my PhD work at Indiana University in 1990, I was also a full-time tenure-track instructor at Jefferson Community College in Louisville, KY, and had been teaching six courses per term (two each from three different institutions in the Louisville area) since 1987. So, at JCC, I taught four composition courses per term (primarily English 101 and 102), along with extensive community service and community education. I commuted to IU for four years to do coursework, took one year to get ready for comps, and then I took an additional two years to write the dissertation. At JCC, while I worked on a degree in literature from IU, most of my colleagues did PhD work in rhetoric and composition at the University of Louisville. I learned under their tutelage that there was an actual writing process that could bring some conceptual order and logical structure to what I'd been thrashing at on my own for years.

Lesson Four

KEY: There is such a thing as "the writing process"!

PROCESS: Writing generally involves three recursive stages: inventing, drafting, and polishing. Each of these stages carries with it a series of identifiable and practical skills that can be taught and learned. Break down longer projects into doable chunklets.

TECHNOLOGY: Apple II, Apple IIe, and Apple III; DOS-based IBM clones.

STORAGE SYSTEM: 5¼-inch disks; Xerox copies & the first file cabinets.

Being recently married in 1989, with two young boys by 1994, my time was at a premium, and so I did my PhD work from 10:00 P.M. to 2:00 A.M. most nights during those years, leaving my best time for the boys. And in 1990, as I've recounted in another place, I found myself trying to comfort my colicky five-month-old son Sam during my first semester of PhD work. I held *The Riverside Chaucer* in one hand and *Dr. Spock's Baby and Child Care* in the other—all in the context of reading Don DeLillo's *White Noise* (in a course with Paul Strohm) and its transcendent chapter 16 that begins, "This was the day Wilder started crying at two in the afternoon"—and I made a decision then to write as much as possible about the things that I was already experiencing and that I was already thinking about. It was for me a matter of both personal efficiency and existential integration, and more than I ever realize I had been writing not only about medieval literature and culture but about my own life and my own need to make sense out of my life.

Lesson Five

KEY: Writing is really about life, not work.

PROCESS: Investigate and integrate the personal and

professional through academic writing.

TECHNOLOGY: IBM PC clone.

STORAGE SYSTEM: 5¼-inch disks; Xerox copies & more file cabinets.

Preeminent in my life since that time has been my experience of being a father, and so that's where I focused my attention in my PhD seminars and what I addressed in my dissertation: children and childhood in Middle English literature and culture. Whenever possible, I wrote my seminar papers on the figure of the child—who in Middle English literature is invariably threatened, killed, or already dead—and so I had the backbone of a New Historicist dissertation in place when I took my comps in the Spring of 1994, when my second son, Jake, was four days old, and I was in a somewhat altered state of consciousness. When I completed my PhD in 1997, I had also achieved tenure in the community college system. I could've stayed put in Louisville, but I went out on the job market for a second year and after getting some really good interviews at top places and a couple of excellent campus visits (but ultimately no offer), I landed a position at the University of Alaska Anchorage, whose hiring schedule then was skewed later in the year than the normal sequence. I signed my contract in June 1997.

Lesson Six

KEY: Align the personal and the professional.

PROCESS: Make every writing task about the same thing—getting the dissertation done and creating opportunities for peer-reviewed publication.

TECHNOLOGY: IBM PC clone.

STORAGE SYSTEM: 5¼-inch disks; Xerox copies & more file cabinets.

1997–2003: Anchorage, from Assistant to Associate

I drove the Al-Can Highway in August 1997, and at UAA, I was brought in with a 4/4 load, with a reasonable service expectation, but no formal research requirement. However, I continued to work toward publication and garnered significant interest from several important university presses for a revision of my dissertation on violence, subjectivity, and medieval children, but a significant personal tragedy derailed those plans but brought my academic work into a personal focus that I could have never anticipated. We lost our third son, Joseph, in the womb in February 1998. In response, Sam and Jake's mom descended into a well of grief that she could negotiate only by self-medicating, and I became essentially a single dad after we broke up in the fall of 2000. In the meantime, in survival mode, and teaching a 4/4 load and three additional courses during the summers, I had to shelve the book and turned instead to piecing out my dissertation in revised articles.

> *Lesson Seven*
>
> KEY: Writing is how I make sense out of a history of trauma and suffering. These are not separate from my writing; they are its substance.
>
> PROCESS: Adapt my writing ambitions to the contours of my life as it is now—not as I dreamed it would be—and it's taken me awhile to reconcile the fact that that is not a failure. There will be no book, but I can write short pieces for specific venues, given my workload and personal responsibilities.
>
> TECHNOLOGY: Windows-based PCs.
>
> STORAGE SYSTEM: 3.5 inch disks; Xerox copies and more file cabinets.

While working toward tenure at UAA (1997–2003), I developed a second, pedagogical track in my writing program, focusing upon the largely novel and rapidly growing uses of the Internet and World Wide Web in higher education and medieval studies. It is now hard to imagine a time before the web (isn't it?), but it was indeed unusual back in the late 1990s and early 2000s in the era of the 14.4k home modem—when web pages were rudimentary, listservs were hip, MUDs were the latest thing, and digital imaging not much better than 8-bit. Web resources were for the first time easily available at my desktop, and I found that much of my academic writing was in fact rewriting (dissertation chapters for specific venues, often without a firm deadline) and opportunistic (based upon chances I found through networking with friends and colleagues, on academic listservs, or online venues like the venerable cfp.english.upenn.edu), and I turned my attention to compiling web-based resources for my Alaskan students of medieval literature, *The Electronic Canterbury Tales* and *The Chaucer Pedagogy Page* (www.kankedort.net), a Web 1.0 resource—part of the *Chaucer Metapage* project—that has languished since 2008 (when Microsoft eliminated FrontPage, the software I'd used to design it). With my tenure application, I successfully argued for a 3/4 (since I was already publishing), which would then incorporate both service and research (formally) into my workload. And it has ever been thus. But really, the days I used to spend researching in libraries I now can take in writing and revising. Because of my location and the vagaries of institutional support, consistent and sustained travel to research libraries and manuscript archives became impossible. Besides, being a dad was more important and better.

Lesson Eight

KEY: Google, 1998. That is all.[1]

PROCESS: I've now got tenure. I can write about ME
literature and culture, and I can write about
pedagogy.

TECHNOLOGY: Windows-based PCs.

STORAGE SYSTEM: 3.5-inch drives and then Zip drives
and omygodthefilecabinetsandfileboxeswhere-
doIputitall.

2003–2010: Anchorage, from Associate to Full

As my boys grew up as digital natives—and I moved from
Associate to Full Professor—their enthusiasms became my
own, and my history as a gamer reaching back to the days of
the Atari 2600 became their obsession with, first, PC games and
ultimately an entire lineage of gaming consoles and increasingly
sophisticated digital games. Oh the games we played! At first, I
was better. Soon, I was not and became cannon fodder for them.
Then, Oh the games I watched them play! My second line of
pedagogical writing blossomed into a third track of research on
neomedievalism in its many guises, particularly digital gaming. Because I see myself first and foremost as a teacher, I'm
constantly thinking about—and trying to find—ways to build
pedagogical bridges between the experiences and enthusiasms
students bring into the classroom and the material I teach. TV
and film are rich sources of complementary material to open up
the classroom to medieval material, but gaming introduces some-

---

1   As I write this paragraph, I'm realizing that I completed all my formal
    educational work before the real advent of the web. I never used the web
    for research for any of my degrees. It seems unthinkable now. Lord, but
    don't I feel like a dinosaur. I belong in a museum.

thing new and different to the discussion of how the contemporary world constantly appropriates and refashions the tropes, characters, narratives, and images of the medieval period. I fell in love, got remarried, and moved out to Wasilla, Alaska, just in time for John McCain to tap Sarah Palin, a Wasilla native and former mayor, as his 2008 running mate, making a little town thirty-five miles north of Anchorage the epicenter of the political universe for a moment. Additionally, as MA program coordinator at UAA at this time, I helped our program to jettison the multi-chapter MA thesis (the mini-dissertation), and developed a thesis proposal course for our MA students to prepare them to write an article-length essay directed toward a specific journal. I had to think again about how to teach composition at a different level, now with MA students, and found myself cleaving to Joseph Williams's *Style: Lessons in Clarity and Grace* to streamline my own academic writing and to teach graduate students to value (and practice) clarity over complexity. Finally, Facebook and the rise of social media create new ways of collaborating, networking, and forming community. Again, I write about what I experience myself and with my boys but move now freely between three different areas of interest: criticism of Middle English texts, pedagogical issues, and digital medievalism.

Lesson Nine

KEY: Learning to say no.

PROCESS: A new and broader range of audiences and resources. Social media posts—sometimes knowingly, sometimes unwittingly—become the first draft of many projects.

TECHNOLOGY: Apple iMac (a switch I made in 2009 and should've made a decade earlier); flip phone.

STORAGE SYSTEM: jump drives, multiple portable backup drives, and a room dedicated to paper files.

2010–15: Anchorage

In 2010, I became Chair of English, and much of my time is now devoted to the nuts and bolts of helping the department run smoothly. While my research productivity has declined, I write more than ever: assessment reports, student learning and program learning outcomes, 1000 emails per month, and all the other institutional and service work that remains hidden to those outside. When I was ejected from my second marriage in Fall 2012, I dumped all but a handful of paper files at the Palmer, Alaska, waste transfer station—1200 lbs in all. I can carry my current research on a jump drive and synch to multiple devices via Cloud computing. In July 2015, I became Director of English, now with supervisory, budgetary, and signatory authority. I attended a recent Association of Departments of English workshop for new administrators, and the draft program the ADE circulated ahead of time included a concurrent session on "Maintaining a Research Profile." When I got to the training in Kansas City, I discovered that this particular session no longer appeared in the list of concurrent sessions. When I asked the organizers about it, they just laughed knowingly. And so I stand here at midcareer, a better writer (I think) than I've ever been but with new and important choices to make: What kind of writing shall I do to continue to make sense of my life as it continues to change? My hunch is that now I'll add a fourth track to the other three and write about the move into administration and the challenges that face the humanities and liberal arts in the continued corporatization of US higher education.

Some people can write while reclining on a couch or slouched in a comfy chair; others can write at a coffee shop or on a layover between flights. I cannot. Some need specific things within their writing environment. I do not. I'm not so picky anymore, except for this: I have to be sitting upright at a desk, preferably with a desktop with a mouse rather than a laptop with a trackpad.

> *Lesson Nine*
> KEY: Turn administrative duties into a fourth track of academic writing.
> PROCESS: Commit to a variety of writing projects with different timelines so that I have to adapt and produce, as I have done in the past.
> TECHNOLOGY: iMac, MacBook Pro, Android Galaxy Tablet, iPhone, Google Calendar; Facebook, Twitter.
> STORAGE SYSTEM: Everything synched to Dropbox Pro via the Cloud.

Looking Ahead

I write all the damn time. I am writing. *All. The. Damn. Time.* I have always already been writing ATDT. And when I'm not writing, and my attention isn't immediately preoccupied with something that needs attention *right now*, I'm usually thinking about writing. Or what I should be writing. Or what I'm going to write. Or what I should be planning to write. Or how am I going to meet that deadline. Or how I really should've written that other part of that other thing from before. And I've added to the prewriting/drafting/revising triad a *planning* phase before and a *shepherding* phase after. Here's an inventory of my current projects, administrative and academic:

A budget criteria document for the Office of Academic
Affairs (committee).

A strategic plan for the Department of English
(committee).

Two book reviews (one late, one very, very late).

One article manuscript review (due in four weeks).

One substantive blog post (due in 4–6 weeks).

A plenary address for the last week of July (will have to
draft at the conference).

Two anthologies (one at the CFP stage and one at the
planning stage).

One co-edited anthology (in the planning stages).

One online collaborative project (in the planning stage).

Two brief essays (due in two weeks).

One major essay (due in six weeks).

One conference paper (due in 10 weeks).

Another conference presentation (due in one year).

Two essays at the shepherding stage.

And, sadly, I often think of those articles and projects that
lay incomplete, at this point only as digital fragments in a
Dropbox folder. Things I've thought about, started, drafted up
to a point, and then never have (yet) finished: youth and age
in *Sir Gawain and the Green Knight*, the figure of the child in
The Canterbury Tales, that synthetic overview of the Middle
English *Abraham and Isaac* plays, and the never-finished "big
book" that haunts me. But when I look back I want to see that
I have had not just a writing career but a writing life.

Here's the first thing I wrote by hand when I started writing
this piece three days ago:

I know my work is done when I hate it. When I'm
convinced it's the most obvious thing in the world. That
anyone could see it and articulate it better than I could.

A child could better. When I'm sure it's the worst thing that's ever been written. Then I know I'm done. It used to bother me—a lot—this feeling of fear and self-loathing. Now I know it's just part of the emotional conclusion of my writing process. When I hate it, I know I'm done, and it's finished.

I feel that way at this moment with this piece, and though I know there is much more to do to make it right, I'm going to submit it to keep with the rough and tumble approach to this volume. But the same old fears are there. I've just made peace with it as part of the process.

If living in Alaska has taught me anything, it's that there's a natural ebb and flow to the currents of life and of nature, of waning light and waxing darkness, and that these cycles cannot be resisted. One must adapt.

I'll end with this.

Lesson Ten
KEY: Always proofread. Just one more time.
PROCESS: Trust me.
TECHNOLOGY: Eye balls.
STORAGE SYSTEM: Inadequate.

My first peer-reviewed article was published when I was a second-year PhD student at IU. Larry Clopper liked a little essay I'd written for his medieval drama seminar on the Jesus and the Doctors plays, and he suggested *Comparative Drama*. I said okay. This was in the era of linotype printing and tear-sheet proofs, and when the essay came out in Winter 1992–93, I excitedly brought an offprint to my cohort at IU. Beaming, I showed them the offprint, which my friends flipped through admiringly, until one of them said, "What's this?" This is what he saw:

Comparative Drama

Joseph, and the three doctors. Rather than being dull and pedantic or simply rehearsing a Christianized version of the Ten Commandments,[17] these Jesus and the Doctors plays each represent the prophesied Savior as a unique and fully articulated character who acts on his own behalf, affects others through his language, and engenders community through his presence,

NOTES

Yes, the end of the beginning of my academic publishing career concluded not with a period, but with a comma,

An error.

Made in the USA
Monee, IL
11 August 2020

37960021R00101